Nine
Lives

The Enneagram in Life Stories

T0095896

Nine
Lives

The Enneagram in Life Stories

Eric Foggitt

BOOKS

Winchester, UK
Washington, USA

First published by O-Books, 2012
O-Books is an imprint of John Hunt Publishing Ltd., Laurel House, Station Approach,
Alresford, Hants, SO24 9JH, UK
office1@jhpbooks.net
www.johnhuntpublishing.com

For distributor details and how to order please visit the 'Ordering' section on our website.

Text copyright: Eric Foggitt 2012

ISBN: 978 1 78099 978 4

A CIP catalogue record for this book is available from the British Library.

Design: Stuart Davies

Printed and bound by CPI Group (UK) Ltd, Croydon, CR0 4YY

We operate a distinctive and ethical publishing philosophy in all
areas of our business, from our global network of authors to
production and worldwide distribution.

CONTENTS

Introduction

One of the oldest pieces of psychological advice is also one of the shortest: *"Know thyself."*[1] It's a simple statement, but extremely deep. Most of us are conscious of a 'real me' somewhere deep inside. That real person doesn't easily get angry, doesn't feel ashamed or get anxious in the way the outer person does, but instead is able to be honest, loving and free. And yet time and again we somehow don't let that 'real me' take charge, so instead we're short-tempered or critical; we find it nigh on impossible to learn from our mistakes. It seems like the 'real me' has a heck of a job kicking out the fake one! This book is about nine people stuck in that rut and how they broke the cycle and grew.

The nine life stories in this book refer to the Enneagram. This is a way of understanding personality (and a whole lot of other things besides, by the way). The roots of the Enneagram are very ancient: we find them in the Bible, (in **Deuteronomy**[2] and elsewhere) and in ancient Egyptian culture. They pop up in the history of the Christian church in a thinker called Evagrius in the 4th century and again in the 13th century with Thomas Aquinas. More recently psychologists such as Freud and Jung have had a deep impact on Enneagram thinking and some newer terms have been added to the topic. Understanding personality, someone once said, is like pinning jelly to the wall, so anything that can help us is welcome!

You may find it interesting and helpful to learn a little about the Enneagram as you read the stories, or afterwards. The website I recommend is www.enneagraminstitute.com, which is full of background and clear descriptions of the types, applications in various areas of life and links to further discussion and research papers.

The Enneagram suggests that there are nine types of personality, or nine ways of seeing the world, or we might even say nine ways we are wired up internally. There are loving and caring people, for instance. Then there are highly sensitive and artistic folk who seem to be quite 'deep'. Then again there are overactive pleasure-seekers and so on. It's fairly easy to describe people's behavior, but what the Enneagram tries to do is get inside and uncover the motivations, drives and passions behind the actions. It suggests, in fact, that each type is trying to deal with a fear – of being unloved, or anonymous, or trapped – any one of the nine basic fears that can afflict us. Don Riso writes:

> Each personality type is an unwitting strategy for escaping from inner pain by pretending it isn't there, by compensating for it in dangerous and destructive ways, by turning to others to solve it, or by being driven so relentlessly that we burn ourselves out rather than experience it directly.[3]

According to Enneagram thinking, most of us are very poor at understanding ourselves. In years of working with the Enneagram in groups and with individuals, I have found that most people have limited insight into themselves. We often think that we are better than we are. We want to believe that the mask we wear for others is actually real. Without some pretty hard work, we lack even a basic understanding of ourselves. But with real devotion to the task, change and positive growth are possible. As Marianne Williamson writes:

> *When Michelangelo was asked how he created a piece of sculpture, he answered that the statue already existed within the marble… Michelangelo's job, as he saw it, was to get rid of the excess marble that surrounded God's creation.*
>
> *So it is with you. The perfect you isn't something you need to create, because God already created it… Your job is to allow the Holy Spirit to remove the fearful thinking that surrounds your perfect self.*"[4]

So these stories – in each one the central figure is a different Enneagram type – are meant to help you understand others and yourself. There are a good few Bible quotes and most of the characters have something to do with church. This is because the Bible says a great deal about character and change. Church can be a place of personal honesty and real growth. If you have a different faith, or none, you shouldn't find the religious content off-putting.

I hope that at least one of the stories will prompt you to say, "Yes, I'm like that!" and most of the others will remind you of people you know. To know others better is also a real grace: it helps us to form healthier relationships and to accept one another as we are, rather than grumble that people are different from us. At the end of each chapter are some ideas for exercises to help you deepen your understanding and then to move on towards finding and nurturing the 'real you', the healthy and mature person whom God wants you to be.

Tim's Story: Type 5

When I consider your heavens,
the work of your fingers,
the moon and the stars,
which you have set in place,
what is mankind that you are mindful of them,
human beings that you care for them?
Psalm 8:3–4

Halfway through the second hymn, young Tim noticed that he could hear flapping noises when different notes were played on the organ. He had seen the pipes and realized some weeks previously that air came blowing out of them, but now another piece of the jigsaw fell into place: by pressing the black and white keys, the organist could open and close the pipes he wanted air to go through! To his 6-year old mind, this came as a wonderful discovery.

Tim's passion is to understand how things work. But when, the following week, the organist was found behind the organ keyboard in the crushing space below the pipes, with Tim pressed hard against his legs, there was a momentary panic among those who observed it. Tim's mother, initially simply relieved to have found her son, broke the tension with laughter when she understood how the situation had been misconstrued. The organist appeared, flushed with the effort of dragging his rather rotund body out of the restricted space and embarrassment at what his observers had been thinking.

"I was er… showing Tim the inside of the organ. He er… asked me how it worked and I…" Tim's mother's laughter was like a hooter echoing around the church.

"Oh, Mr. Simpson, that was so kind of you –"she began, once she had subdued her laughter. "He was on about it all week." She

4

was actually genuinely delighted that the organist had put her out of her misery, because once Tim got thinking about something, it was like a broken record – the same thing again and again – until he understood, or got bored. But Mr. Simpson made an internal note to himself about undertaking well-intentioned deeds with young children.

In the second half of primary school when, he noticed, three of his friends worked out that there were no dinosaurs in the Bible and gave this as a reason to stop going to church, he came to a different conclusion – with a little help from his father.

"Why are there no dinosaurs in the Bible?" he had asked him, flatly.

"Well, I guess because the people who wrote the Bible didn't know about them, so they didn't ask God about them. Maybe the guy who wrote Genesis got told to write about dinosaurs, but didn't know what they were, so he didn't. I don't know really... Does it matter?"

"It matters," said 10-year old Tim, "because some bits don't kinda fit. Like God being angry in the Old Testament and loving in the New Testament."

"It's not quite like that, but I know what you mean," his father replied.

"So how do you fit everything together?" Tim asked, quite anxious now.

His father didn't reply for almost a minute, and then responded quietly: "Y'know, Tim, some things work out in different ways. Not everything works like numbers that add up. Some things have a logic all of their own."

It was like hearing the organ flaps working four years previously in the church. But this time a bigger section of the jigsaw clicked into place. Tim found it wonderful that there could be different types of thinking.

By that beautiful and mysterious understanding that exists between some children and their parents, his father sensed where his son was at with this and added: "Imagine you couldn't see red, you didn't have the ability to see red. Think of all the things you couldn't see... strawberries, raspberries... red roses and tulips... blood... Mars! You couldn't see these things until somehow you learned how to see red. And some bits of life are like that: your brain's great for working out how machines work, but it needs to work kinda differently to make out how the Bible all fits together."

By now Tim was thrilled to the point of agitation and his eyes were wide open and staring at his father. "You mean God thinks in a different way from us?"

"Exactly!" said his father triumphantly. He was suddenly very proud of his son – and of his own parenting skills.

That evening he scanned through the pages of Isaiah and underlined a passage which he would show his son the next day:

"For my thoughts are not your thoughts,
neither are your ways my ways," declares the LORD.
"As the heavens are higher than the earth,
so are my ways higher than your ways
and my thoughts than your thoughts."
Isaiah 55:8–9

As he grew up, Tim's bedroom was his retreat and safe-place – so much so that his mother sometimes commented to her friends about her concerns that he was becoming isolated and friendless. She often felt excluded from his real life, as if he was deliberately cutting himself off from her. But Tim often felt she was making demands on his which he couldn't meet, and sometimes even had a dream in which little parts of him were being eaten by others – like a fish being nibbled by a piranha. He was confounded by the 'real world' outside whereas in his bedroom he could work things out and think without interruptions from his parents and his younger sister. Only his father could sometimes enter that private world, because he seemed to have an insight into the way Tim thought about things.

When his school friends stopped attending church and Sunday school, Tim was unconcerned. He loved the weird and wonderful stories in the Old Testament and, far from being influenced by their growing skepticism, became increasingly interested in the 'other world' of miracles and secret knowledge. His father once commented that if there had been a Masonic club for children, Tim would have joined it.

At university, where he studied computing, for the first time in his life Tim met with several people with similar interests and who seemed to think the way he did. They would talk for hours about some obscure topic to do with computing, programming or configuration. Gradually he became almost contemptuous of the 'ordinary' students around him, who all did the same things, dressed the same way and didn't think much about anything.

His faith was like a private room deep within him, and he found it almost impossible to explain what or why he believed to others. For several months one verse from a letter of Paul's went round and round in his mind:

... the mystery that has been kept hidden for ages and generations, but is now disclosed to the Lord's people.
Colossians 1:26

He was intrigued with the idea that some people – and he considered himself to be one of them – had been given this secret awareness, while others had not. It explained for Tim why most of the people he knew at university had no faith.

He scanned chapters of Paul's other letters and came upon:

... God's grace that was given to me for you, that is, the mystery made known to me by revelation, as I have already written briefly. In reading this, then, you will be able to

7

understand my insight into the mystery of Christ.
Ephesians 3:2–4

Weeks went past during which he read and re-read these words, memorizing them as he did so. The thought then struck him that the whole idea would have more force if he could find it elsewhere in the Bible, in the words of Jesus for instance. So he began speed-reading the gospels and he was not even halfway through Matthew's gospel when he came upon:

"I praise you, Father, Lord of heaven and earth, because you have hidden these things from the wise and learned, and revealed them to little children..."
Matthew 11:25

Jesus spoke cryptically about his parables, sometimes suggesting that their cryptic nature prompted his listeners either to reject his words as nonsense, or to go deeper by reflecting more about their hidden meaning, even quoting Isaiah as he did so:

Though seeing, they do not see;
though hearing, they do not hear or understand.
Matthew 13:13

Yet as Tim delved deeper – as he saw it – into the mysteries of the Bible, even visiting Patmos one Easter holiday in order to explore the cave where John received the revelation which forms the last book of the Bible, it was as if he had become infatuated with the mystery rather than understood its meaning and impact. The obscurities of John's writing fed his hunger for mental challenges. The sense which this gave him that he was in a tiny minority with privileged insight reinforced his view that he was unlike ordinary mortals, who neither understood these mysteries nor even looked into them. Yet he could see within himself that his interest in the obscure and recondite far outweighed his desire to unravel the obscure threads and dark themes of this part of the Bible. He marveled in the inscrutability of it all.

Even as he sat on the boat heading back to Piraeus from Patmos, surrounded by dozens of other young adults – mostly American, it has to be said – he had no desire to discuss his experiences with them or discover theirs. He realized that he must sometimes appear to be detached and distant from people, perhaps to the point of looking a bit superior or even proud, but if so it was an appearance which served him well: he wasn't really a people person.

(It is striking how rarely we observe ourselves justifying and rationalizing our oddities and mistakes, because the cleverness we deploy to do so could, one would imagine, be more profitably used to gain insight into our hidden motives. Tim's happy social isolation reduced still further the chances that he would be helped out of his social awkwardness by a friend's useful comment or even a critic's biting complaint.)

Almost the only exception to this was Catherine, the pastor's daughter, whom he found easy and fun company. He didn't have to pretend to be sociable with her; when they were together it was as if they were playing a game, as they had done at school. He loved the way she broke social rules – she had sat on his lap with her arm around his neck as she explained that she was getting married to Sandy, her rich businessman friend.

During his last year at University he was invited to visit an insurance company back home with a view to working in the IT department. His guide on that day was a young man called Keith who was a year or so older than him and who had recently started attending Tim's church. Keith had an austere kind of manner and Tim was unnerved by the sense that he was being appraised and judged. He decided that he would avoid him as much as possible. Keith, for his part, saw Tim as nervous and secretive. He was clearly very able and skilled in computing, but somewhat nerdy and even a bit weird: he decided he couldn't really trust him. He went home and found a bible verse which he decided was intended for the likes of Tim:

We know that "We all possess knowledge."
But knowledge puffs up while love builds up.
1 Corinthians 8:1

Less than three months after starting work, his boss suffered a heart attack and took early retirement. Tim was amazed to be asked to take over leading the small department, but did so almost without question. Quickly his office became a new hideaway for him and as the years passed, so the walls around him became firmer and ever less penetrable.

You have searched me, LORD, and you know me.
You know when I sit and when I rise;
you perceive my thoughts from afar.
You discern my going out and my lying down;
you are familiar with all my ways.
Before a word is on my tongue you, LORD, know it
completely.
You hem me in behind and before, and you lay your hand
upon me.
Such knowledge is too wonderful for me,
too lofty for me to attain.
Psalm 139:1–6

Catherine was smiling at him from across the gym. They had met on numerous occasions since they had left school together, but recently he hadn't seen much of her. Word in the church had it that she and her husband were having marital problems, which must be pretty tough for her as the pastor's daughter.

Tim smiled back, but didn't move from the cross trainer

machine he was sweating on. A moment later Catherine appeared and stood in front of him. He liked the way she flirted with him. She enjoyed trying to provoke him out of his usual distant and detached manner. As he looked at her, he thought to himself that she didn't behave the pastor's married daughter – she was much too forward and provocative, as she had always been. But nor did she look upset by marriage difficulties: Tim concluded that what he had overheard after the last deacon's meeting must just be gossip.

"Hey, Timmy Thompson, meet you downstairs half an hour!" and with that she swept away, pausing briefly to wink at him over her shoulder.

Tim didn't understand how these boy-girl relationship things worked. As a teenager he had often blushed painfully when he talked to girls, a fact that Catherine (or Katie as everyone knew her then) enjoyed exploiting, usually in front of other girls. Once she had told him that he was handsome in a geeky kind of way, and he had been so embarrassed he had avoided her for nearly a month after that. But secretly he was delighted she had said it.

"You're late." She was sitting in the middle of the café with a large iced latte.

"Showers were all taken. Men take so long to wash. I think some of them like to stand there and show off."

"Really? Do men do that?" she giggled. Tim, observing her behavior, told himself there were definitely no marriage problems. He sensed his mood tumbling and his gaze drifted away from Catherine. "Anyway," she went on, changing the subject quickly, "is there lots of gossip about me and Sandy?"

"I – " Tim began, then paused as he questioned himself about how much he should know, and whether he should believe what he had heard, and whether he should admit that he had been listening, in case that revealed why he was interested.

Catherine laughed. "Hey, it's OK. You don't get to be a PK without learning the ground rules."

"A PK?"

"Pastor's kid. We don't talk about what Dad says at home, we don't tell him what everyone says about him at church. Ground rule number one."

"Yes, I heard you were having problems."

"Sandy's left me. Gone to be with his bit of stuff."

"Oh no. I really – " Tim knew that he was out of his depth and he became aware that there were feelings floating around which he couldn't begin to understand. It was an awareness which made him suddenly anxious.

"Hey, it's OK. It's been a long time coming and we both saw it a while back. Matter of fact, it's good now. I feel really high! It's like being a teenager again. Freedom."

It was this sense of fun which Tim had always found irresistible about Catherine; that, and the fact that she flirted openly with him. He looked at her as she laughed about her newfound freedom and he also realized that he found her very sexually attractive. He mentally scratched around to think about what to say. Finally he mumbled, "Must be hard splitting up when you're the pastor's daughter."

For a long while Catherine looked at Tim and, surprised out of her euphoria by Tim's unexpectedly insightful comment, she realized that Tim had given her breakup a lot of thought. She knew that usually he wasn't one to dwell on people's feelings, or to try to feel things from someone else's point of view. She felt suddenly privileged.

"It's really kind of you to say that," she said, seriously. "Most people seem to think that it's just wrong for us to split up, so I'm the bad girl." She paused and looked at him for so long he squirmed and looked away.

"I really like you, Tim," she said, unconcerned that her words would embarrass him hugely.

The last thing Tim could do – look at her – was the very thing he was longing to do as he took in what she had said. His mind became a torrent of thoughts about Catherine and her marriage to Sandy, his desire to be with her, and what he should now say. He swallowed hard, but no words came. His thoughts, tumbling over one another, were dizzy and disordered. Finally he thought that what he was doing now – chatting up a married woman who was going through a marital problem – was decidedly improper. He took hold of his bag and got up, as if that thought had been conclusive – which it hadn't.

"I've got to go. I'm going to be late. It was lovely seeing you." He had nothing pressing to do, but he had suddenly found it stressful being with Catherine. She was like an overactive child who was at any time likely to fall and do injury to herself and others. Besides, he needed to straighten out his thoughts about her.

"Can I drop by some time?" she asked, once his back was turned and he was striding away. He slowed almost to a halt, and nodded his head vigorously without looking round.

Tim was very fond of Catherine. In addition to the sexual attraction, he loved her sense of freedom and her readiness to do daring, cheeky and adventurous things. He felt drawn to her also because deep down inside he sensed that there was a lot about her which would be good for him. But the idea of a relationship with her, even a brief fling, was scary. Tim was far too serious a young man to have brief flings anyway, but if he had been less afraid and he had been forced into a fling with someone, then it would have been with Catherine. He had fantasized about having sex with Catherine, but his mental scenarios were always devoid of conversation; they would be in bed or in a field or a river and their passion would be wordlessly powerful. In fifth year at school he had read *Wuthering Heights* and he had found Heathcliff to be much less strange than the teacher had suggested. Tim had no idea how to establish, still less maintain, a boy-girl relationship and the reality was, intimacy threatened him. He thought that a close relationship would smother him, both because he didn't know how these things worked, but also because he found it difficult to express his feelings and wishes. If he went on a date – he had only ever been on three and each had lasted just one night – he insisted on letting the girl decide where they would go and what they would do. It was easier that way. But he felt none the less swamped and dominated; the language of relationships was a foreign one and Tim was no linguist.

More to the point, he couldn't understand why people spent so much time and energy on chatting up, dating and so on. When he sorted out a complicated software problem he got a great sense of satisfaction; it was an achievement and he felt more competent and useful. But what, precisely, was the reward in a relationship? Why would he want to spend so much time and effort for something which was so meagerly rewarding? Waiting for the dentist once he had found a little quote on the 'agony aunt' page: "Sex is the price women pay for marriage. Marriage the price men pay for sex." And then, as the dentist searched in vain for signs of decay in his mouth, Tim decided that he wholly agreed with the agony aunt but it was way too dear a price for him to pay for sex.

He often felt safer with Catherine because they had known each other a long time – since first year at secondary school, in fact – and because when they were together it was like children playing. He knew that she knew that he was attracted to her and she teased him. But she knew that he knew that she would never so much as kiss him on the cheek. Once, on a school geography trip, she had sat on his knee the whole way back and they had talked about rocks and sediment and geology and he had felt like a million dollars because there were others on the bus who fancied Katie McCreadie but she had chosen to be with him. He had no idea that she wanted to kiss him and be held by him; nor that for two months afterwards she had been able to think of no one else. Half the class had seen the clues and read the obvious signs; eventually one of Katie's friends told Tim, but he instantly dismissed it with a shy laugh as another of the wind-ups and hoaxes which his awkwardness laid him open to.

Therefore when Catherine had uttered those words "I really like you, Tim" he had completely missed the subtext: "I'm in a mess right now and I need your closeness; show me love." She was offering herself to him but he was quite unaware. All he heard was a teasing reminder of the flirty times they had had as school kids and he recognized the strong potential for embarrassment.

At work the following Monday he had to sort out a major software problem. A new application which the marketing department had bought and was using was creating occasional conflicts with the intranet. He cursed himself for agreeing to the purchase of it some months ago; they had pressured him into a quick decision in order to benefit from a price promotion and he hadn't had time to check it out as thoroughly as he usually did. He started work on it a little after half past eight.

Lunchtime came and went and he barely noticed. He put right several glitches in the application which were clearly irrelevant to the conflict, but they had annoyed him so he was glad to have put them right. Around four o'clock he found the problem in a default setting; it would need to be re-written. It took him another hour to gain access to the code. Meticulously he read it to himself, ignoring the telephone ringing and two prolonged sets of knocks at his locked door. Briefly it occurred to him that a fire alarm might have gone off, but he dismissed the idea and continued with his work. The writers of this program had been very lazy and used three chunks of code which had several potential conflicts within them. They were probably irrelevant to the problem he faced, but he carefully re-wrote them and when he saw the long pages of code which he was able to delete as a result, simplifying that part of the program greatly, he was buzzing with joy.

The lights went out in the offices and corridor adjacent to his and Tim failed to notice. He was getting more and more excited at the resolution of the conflict problem.

He felt his stomach rumbling with hunger – he had eaten only two muesli bars all day – and wondered what his mother had prepared for tea. (His parents were at that moment eating it and wondering where Tim was.) He told himself that after he had finished he would need to get the revised version uploaded onto all the marketing computers – no small job in itself, since they were all so devoid of computer literacy: he would probably have to do it himself in the morning before they came in to work.

He reached the last section of the program and read it through in minute detail. The problem had been caused by five different sections conflicting not only with the intranet software, but with each other. No wonder the company making it had sold it off cheap: they had had to re-write it all anyway! He closed off the program and glanced up at the clock above his door. Surely that was impossible: quarter to nine? He told himself that it must have stopped. When he looked outside he saw that it was dark and the street lights were shining brightly. He was genuinely astonished that the whole working day and more had passed so quickly.

When he reflected on church and his relationships with people there, Tim occasionally thought about his affinity to the Old Testament prophets such as Jeremiah and Hosea – men who stood outside society somewhat and offered a godly criticism of its failings. At deacons' meetings especially he felt like this, and three times over the past year he made only one comment during a discussion but it had been the decisive contribution each time and had swung the argument. After the second of these, the pastor stopped him as he was preparing to leave.

"Thanks for your comment, Tim. It was very helpful."

"No problem."

"You have a way of thinking from outside the box sometimes. You like mental puzzles, don't you?"

Tim smiled. The pastor handed him an envelope. "Read it

when you get home. See if you can work it out."

Before he got on his bike he opened the envelope and read.

You're not a Tim but a Jerry. You're not a 2, but a 5.

His immediate thought was that the pastor had written Tim instead of Tom, referring to the old cat and mouse cartoons in his childhood, but he quickly discarded that thought. And why should he be a number? And why not a 2, but a 5? And who was Jerry?

He desperately wanted solve the riddle so that when he saw the pastor at the weekend he could demonstrate his success, but despite wrangling with the words almost every waking hour, he got no further than associating Jerry with Jeremiah and Tim with Paul's helper and disciple, Timothy.

When he revealed this to the pastor, his response was to ask about the 2 and the 5.

"I have no idea whatsoever. How can I be a 5? Or a 2?"

"Speak to Keith."

If Tim had been a 2 he would probably have instantly seen this for what it was – a ploy to get him talking to the one person he really didn't get on with at all in the church, and who didn't like him. The notion that he would go asking that man for personal information was revolting. He looked like he washed himself in bleach every morning and he had teeth like a Hollywood film star. But when two weeks had gone by and he was losing sleep at night trying to work it out, he resolved that he would have to do so. Then, as he was drifting into sleep, he woke and sat up in bed.

He took hold of his laptop from the foot of his bed and started it up. Quickly, he typed "personality numbers" into Google. The search machine provided him with the answer to the pastor's riddle, and he sent him a triumphant e-mail at once announcing his success.

The pastor had hoped that this discovery would lead to Tim going further with this Enneagram thinking and looking into himself, but he was disappointed. Tim was not interested in himself as an issue or topic for analysis and if he had realized that the pastor was urging him to engage on this inner quest, he might well have stopped going to church – such was his fear of others' demands.

When Catherine turned up one evening Tim knew nothing of it for well over an hour, as his father had engaged her in conversation. He had known her from her earliest childhood and as she grew up within the fellowship of the church he admired her energy and sense of fun. Tim, who was deep in thought as he read a scholarly book about symbols used in apocalyptic writing in the Bible, had forgotten that she had suggested she might visit.

He had been so deep in reflection that he initially hardly noticed her knock at the bedroom door. He came to with a broad smile and he led her to the conservatory off the kitchen. Even Catherine was excluded from his bedroom fortress.

"So how is it living with your parents?" she asked.

"Cool," he responded, flatly and then added: "I leave them alone and they leave me alone. I pay rent; everyone's happy. My mum thinks I'm not safe to live alone!"

They sat at opposite ends of the wickerwork sofa, she sitting facing him with her knees tucked up; he turned only slightly towards her.

"How's it going with your man?" Tim couldn't remember her husband's name and felt embarrassed not being able to say it. The thought occurred to him that Catherine might take this as an expression of dislike, or envy.

"Oh no, he's left for good. He wants kids and he wants them like now!" She could sometimes blurt out private truths in a way that offended people, but Tim took it matter-of-factly and in his stride.

"And you're not into kids?"

"Not for now..."

They talked for an hour before Tim's mother appeared with a

trolley laden with a large teapot and a plate of scones. "Thought you might need some supplies," she explained. "Would you prefer a cold drink, Katie? Tim's a tea addict."

"No, tea's fine. Thanks." When Tim's mother had left the room Catherine commented: "She's such a 2!"

Without reflection, Tim immediately said: "Your dad says I'm not a 2 but a 5."

"Which is pretty obvious," she replied. "Did you read more about it, do the test or anything?"

"No, I'm not that into it."

As they talked, for perhaps the first time in his adult life Tim didn't feel threatened by intimacy. He was on home ground and in a place of safety and he had known Catherine a long time. She wasn't flirting with him for a change, also.

"I meant what I said at the gym, about really liking you."

"We've been pals for ages," Tim responded, trying to assert safer parameters. "You're like my big sister."

Catherine's heart sank; that wasn't what she wanted to hear. She replied "Yes, I guess I am. What you doing Sunday after church?"

"Not a lot. Why?"

"Fancy going to the gym, then doing lunch?"

"It's a date."

After a pub lunch Catherine drove through the Worcestershire countryside aimlessly, both of them enjoying the warm early summer sun with the car's sunroof open. "Sandy's not getting to keep my toy though!" she shouted as she accelerated away from a crossroads. Tim liked the way Catherine didn't intrude on his inner life and didn't make demands. He felt like a child with her, as if they were playing together. Neither of them spoke until they had stopped at a lay-by overlooking a broad valley. They admired the view.

Tim was at peace. His body tired from a heavy workout at the gym and his mind for once at rest, he felt profoundly present in the moment, as if he were seeing things afresh and with brighter colors than before. Catherine was sitting beside him with her head back and her eyes closed now. Tim drank in the sights all round him without a felt need to reflect, think and work things out. Quietly he gave thanks to God for everything and everyone.

Fifteen minutes passed. Catherine looked at Tim and their eyes met. She half nodded as if to signal that she had sensed the specialness of the moment, and started up the car.

As they neared home, it was Tim who spoke: "Drop me at your house. I'll walk home."

Catherine stopped the car in front of her house and they stepped out. She approached Tim and he opened his arms. He hugged her with a warmth and tenderness which he had felt for years, but had never been able to express before. He held her for what felt like a long time to Catherine, but just a moment to Tim. He continued to hold her slightly at arms' length and looked deep into her eyes. "I love you so much," he began, making a huge effort at intimacy for this dear and close friend. "I want to always be here for you." She felt his platonic intimacy as a kind of rebuke to her desire. Sometimes he was so pure! He went on: "We're great friends, the best of friends." Then he hugged her again, sensing the warmth of her body against his and the gentle touch of her hair against his face. Within his fast-beating heart he sensed that as he held her, he held something of the whole universe around him. The joy he felt deep inside was that he could embrace without needing to understand.

As he walked home along the canal bank Tim resolved not to see Catherine again until she had sorted out her problems with Sandy. He enjoyed being with her, but he could feel that she wanted more from him than he was willing to give. He felt the hard ground below his feet as he strode confidently home and he imagined he was dancing. It was a dance he had often observed, but now he was actually taking part in it and it felt good, so good.

Spiritual Exercises for 5s

1   When you feel overwhelmed by events or experiences, observe yourself retreating into the safety of your own thoughts.

2   *"Love the Lord your God with all your mind, all your heart and all your strength."* For you the first part of this important command will come easily, but what about the 2nd and 3rd parts?

3   What is God saying to you in your heart? Do you listen to him there? When people reveal their emotions what is your reaction? Why?

4   Read a love poem every day for a month. How do they make you feel?

5   What do you do to nurture and develop your body's strength and health? Can you feel your body as a temple of his Holy Spirit?

6   *"Perfect love casts out fear."* "As they talked, for perhaps the first time in his adult life Tim didn't feel threatened by intimacy." What is it about intimacy that makes you fearful?

7   It may well be easy for you to identify an area in which you are an expert. Can you identify an area in which you are rather weak? How could you develop this into a strength?

8   What is it that makes you ashamed? Why?

9   Get involved in a project (at church or elsewhere) in which you can make a contribution and see it through to success. Learn to find practical outlets for your best ideas.

10 Jesus spoke about the Kingdom in terms of being childlike. Pray for this childlike trust and openness for yourself, and that you become aware when you distance yourself and suspect others.

Mary's Story: Type 8

And these signs will accompany those who believe: In my name they will drive out demons; they will speak in new tongues...
Mark 16:17

"Where do you come from?" he asked Jesus, but Jesus gave him no answer. "Do you refuse to speak to me?" Pilate said. "Don't you realize I have power either to free you or to crucify you?" Jesus answered, "You would have no power over me if it were not given to you from above.
John 19:9–11

On Mary's seventh birthday her grandmother gave her a bike – the first one she had owned. Her father immediately promised to take her out and teach her how to ride it, but before the first party guests had left Mary was out on her own in the street with her new toy. The very idea that she needed someone to teach her how to ride it seemed ridiculous to her. And as she slipped onto the saddle and began pedaling she almost burst with pride and a wonderful sense of independence. It was a feeling which lasted all of four seconds, and was replaced by a pain from her bleeding knee and one in her ribs, where the handlebars had dug into her as she fell off. Most other children would have immediately cried out in pain, but Mary simply wiped the wound with the inside of the hem of her birthday dress, and tried again. This time she just managed to stop herself falling to the ground. And so it went on, for twenty minutes. Three times she fell off and hurt herself, but by the time she was ready to head home, she could ride her bike for 20 meters and not a tear had been shed, despite her wounds.

That incident was typical of her childhood: a sense of independence and being in control of things thrilled her, while having to do what she was told or, worse still, watch someone else incompetent mess things up, was almost physically painful. Her brother Simon, who is two years older than her, was often grateful for her protection. He is easy-going and relaxed, always willing to do what others were doing but as a result he sometimes got pushed around. When she was six, she decided that he needed a bit of support on the football field, so she started going with him to play. She was the only girl, and at first the boys sniggered at her lack of skill, but soon their sniggers turned to respectful glances. Her tackles were strong and sometimes painful; the better players started avoiding her, and she started scoring goals. Her brother, in her shadow once again, stopped playing. She loved the challenge of playing against these bigger and older boys, but when other girls turned up she was scornful.

There are some people who seem to have a natural authority. Even before they speak, the way they dress and the way they walk – determined and confidently – indicate that you're dealing with someone who knows what they want and is pretty committed to getting it. Mary was one of them.

A few years ago in her mid twenties she had persuaded herself that her clothes were shrinking: she could think of no other explanation for the way they all seemed so tight on her. Her partner at the time, John, wouldn't have dared tell her the truth. Finally she weighed herself secretly at a friend's house one evening, and the scales told a frightening story that she could scarcely believe: after all, she didn't eat big meals! But her friends and family had all noticed; she had been putting on weight inexorably, as if subconsciously she wanted to grow, in order to express her presence and her strength.

Some years ago Keith invited her to a special church event in a large concert hall in the city. They were in the office canteen at the time – they worked for the same insurance company.

"You're a Sarah Grainsford fan, aren't you, Mary?" he asked, out of the blue.

"Yes, I am. She's in *Streetwise* on the telly. Why?"

"She's speaking at this big church shindig tomorrow night at the Irvine Hall. Talking about losing her husband."

"Yeah, he was only 34. What d'you mean, talking?"

"She's a Christian and she's going to talk about how God helped her through it. I can get you a ticket if you want. There's a gang of us from church going."

Mary sensed a trap. She certainly didn't like the idea of spending an evening with a bunch of religious weirdoes. But she trusted Keith and she had been touched by a short article she had read in a magazine about Sarah Grainsford's husband dying and how she had handled it.

"I've never been to anything like that before. What's it like?"

"I imagine it'll be a bit noisy – "

"Noisy? A church meeting? Will there be like... hymns?" Mary's awareness of church was limited to *Songs of Praise* that she accidentally caught snatches of on the TV.

"There'll be a praise band and lots of fairly noisy music..."

"I can handle that. I'd like to hear what Sarah G. has to say."

"I'll get the ticket to you tomorrow – unless you want to come with us. We're meeting up at the Bull at seven."

"Sure. I'll meet you there."

What Mary admired most about the story Sarah told during the meeting was the way she refused pity and asserted that God alone had given her the ability to get through the grief after her loss. She was intrigued to hear how confident the soap star was about her source of strength. Before hearing her speak she had wondered whether such a tragedy would shake someone's faith, but in Sarah Grainsford's case it seemed to have strengthened it.

Towards the end of the meeting people were invited forward to receive some kind of 'blessing' which, oddly to Mary, consisted of being touched on the forehead and then falling down. To the right of the stage was a cordoned-off area where a group of people including Sarah Grainsford were sitting with people and praying for them. Mary got up and strode down towards the seats and sat down close to where the actress was sitting. After a couple of minutes she found herself face to face with the young woman she had watched many times on *Streetwise*.

"Hi. I'm Sarah. Would you like to tell me your name?"

"I'm Mary." She was a little star-struck.

"What can I pray for you?" asked the soap star.

"I was really moved when you spoke about finding strength in God. I've never experienced that. I guess I've always thought that faith was for weak people, a kinda crutch."

"Well I suppose it can be that sometimes. People use religion for their own purposes, don't they? But God is amazingly powerful."

"I'd really like you to pray for me. I'd like to feel his power."

When Sarah gently held Mary's hand what felt like a torrent of tears flowed from her eyes: she suddenly and unexpectedly recalled a memory of her Aunt Ida dying when Mary was just nine years old. Everyone had said she would cry at the funeral, but she had remained dry-eyed throughout, even when her mother, Ida's sister, had wept. Now, having her hand held by this bereaved actress brought back powerful memories of that event.

"… and I pray that Mary senses your power, Lord God – power to save, to support and to enable her to become all that you want her to become."

She hardly heard anything else that Sarah Grainsford prayed. The idea that she could become someone better and stronger was so deeply and movingly exciting that her tears stopped at once and as she became aware that the actress had stopped praying, so she sensed what felt like a strong electric current flowing through her hand and arm, and into her body.

"Whoa…" Mary cried out, almost jumping up out of her seat. "Thank you so much! I'm really glad I came."

Sarah smiled slightly, and then turned to face another person, leaving Mary with a wonderful warm glow.

The next day, a Saturday, she woke up feeling almost depressed. All the excitement of the previous evening had vanished and Mary felt weak and a bit sad. As she went through the morning she started feeling she had been manipulated. It wasn't fair, she reflected, to use someone like Sarah Grainsford in that way. The fact that she admired her as a soap star had made her vulnerable. Soon her sadness turned to anger. She would speak about it with Keith on Monday, she decided.

Instead of eating lunch, Mary went for a walk along the river. She had never done so before, not alone anyway. More memories of the previous evening came back to her, better ones now. She recalled something Sarah Grainsford had said in her prayer: *"enable her to become all that you want her to become."* The thought that she could become more than she currently was thrilled her once again. And then an idea came into her head and she spoke to it out, quietly, to herself: *What if God really is the source of power?*

Speaking about it afterwards to Keith, Mary claimed that she didn't know why she turned up at the New Life Fellowship on the following Sunday evening, but the truth was she was greedy for more of the wonderful electric feeling she had had two days before, and she was keen to find out more about the God of power that Sarah had prayed about. She wasn't disappointed: she clapped and danced during the praise band songs, and after the message she went forward for prayer. "I want more of God," she simply said, and as hands were laid on her head, she felt the electric warmth running through her once again.

It was matter of just three months before she was the one doing the praying and laying-on of hands. She had been impressed with the pastor's quick acceptance of her, recognizing not only the reality of her faith, but also her gift. She looked and felt confident. Each week at the evening service she would go forward near the end and offer to pray for people – at least, she would lay her right hand on their forehead and they would collapse onto the carpet, helped down by two 'catchers' who stood facing her. She was gripped by the fabulous feeling of being a channel through which God could bless people. She noticed that there would usually be a small queue of people waiting for her, while the other three or four people praying rarely had more than one person waiting. When she went home after the meeting she felt on top of the world, ready for the coming work week.

With her friends Mary was quite open about what had happened, but she put a slight gloss on her reasons for going and being involved in the church. "The people at that church are just really warm and genuine and accepting. And when I pray for people they really do seem to benefit from it." Behind her back they derided her sudden conversion. "It's kind of odd that it happens three months after John dumped her," one said. Mary had often encountered people who didn't like her strength, but she enjoyed being the challenger, especially when she sensed an opportunity to protect someone who was being bullied or exploited. It had happened several times at school, once against a teacher who was subsequently disciplined by the school board. To soften the edge of her energy – she even sensed it herself – she had a developed a soft and gently caring way of speaking which seemed to serve her well. She was successful in her work and her friends knew her as someone who got things done, so even when they felt dominated by her, they admired her and sometimes envied her. But the religious stuff she was now into was a different story; it seemed so sudden and weird to her old friends.

After a few months at the Fellowship the pastor invited her to his house one Saturday lunchtime. To her surprise, she was alone with him: she had thought it was a meeting of some kind. He brought her coffee and they sat in the somewhat Spartan lounge adjacent to each other, speaking for a few minutes about her work, church and worship and coming to faith.

With a slightly embarrassed look, the pastor said, "Actually,

Mary, there's a kind of personal reason I asked you here. I'd really like to take you out for dinner some time, but I want you to pray about whether it's the right thing to do."

Mary smiled at the thought of praying about going on a date: she didn't need to do that! As she listened to him, she reflected that Pastor Richie was a lovely guy that half the single girls in the church would give their right arm to date.

"Oh... well, I'm really touched. I'll er... do that..."

"And of course if you don't think it's right, then in no way will this change anything at church and... er... it would be best if no one else heard about it – if... er it's a 'No'."

A few days later, after the evening church meeting, they went to a quiet pub some eight miles out of town. The date went very well; she was relaxed and chatty, he was ironic and funny. Richie took her home and accompanied her to her front door, where he demurely kissed her on the cheek. She longed to invite him in, but decided that this was not what you did on a first date with a Pentecostal pastor. When she shut the door behind her, and heard his ageing sports car drive off, she saw herself in the hallway mirror, a broad smile on her face.

When Mary thought about it – after only their fourth date – she found the prospect of marrying Ritchie hugely enticing. He wasn't very exciting or sexy, but he was quite good-looking and when she reflected on it their partnership might work really well: she had the drive and the ambition; he had the ideas and the position.

When she told her parents on New Year's Day that she and Richie were to be married, they were taken aback. It had been hard enough for them to take in her newfound enthusiasm for the church, which they had themselves carefully avoided all through her childhood. They had met Richie just once, briefly, when he had brought her home in his car. Mary's father had admired the old MG and chatted briefly with Richie before he headed home again. But they firmly thought that John would reappear on the scene; he had been such a fixture in their daughter's life for so long, they liked him a lot and they had the impression that Richie was a bit of a 'rebound' relationship.

"But you've known each other, what... four months?" asked her mother.

"Six," replied Mary, bending the truth somewhat. It had been barely eight weeks since that first evening at the country pub, six months since she had started attending the church.

"Well, if you're really sure, Mary..." started her father. He was usually the one to give in to her first. "You're old enough to know your own mind, I'm sure."

Thus far in her relationship with Richie, she had seen him as a challenge. She had heard two young women of her age speaking about him very affectionately, and when news of their dating got out, she won admiring glances from several people. But she inwardly considered him a challenge because of what becoming the pastor's wife would mean to her. The spiritual and religious feelings she got from church services were so thrilling that the prospect of being at the very heart of everything in the fellowship was appealing in a way nothing else had been in her life. She loved Richie, but her feelings for him were nothing like what they had been for John. Perhaps that in itself was another good reason she loved him – with John she had such powerful feelings she sometimes felt vulnerable, and she detested that.

They were married on the Saturday of the next Pentecost weekend – a most fitting time to get hitched, several people remarked. Mary's parents sat looking rather bemused through the service, as the band played excitedly and loud and the ageing visiting preacher spoke at some length about the Holy Ghost. They honeymooned in the south of Spain, staying at an expensive golfing hotel which Ritchie's father paid for.

The first sign of trouble in their relationship was at a church leaders' meeting barely six weeks after their marriage.

"The numbers turning out at both services are down by

40–50%," said one.

"The meetings are getting samey and predictable…"

"A number of people are asking questions about Mary: she's a young Christian and she seems to be running things around here." Several of the elders nodded and voiced agreement.

The truth was Richie had found Mary a considerable help to him in his work. She could act confidently where he would appear hesitant and halfhearted. She liked being with people, and even winning over the difficult ones, whereas he was a bit shy and nervous with them. And the crunch issue was that she could tell people what to do; he couldn't. After thinking it through, he concluded that she was the one who could put his ideas into action; they were a great team! The prospect of reducing her involvement, or perhaps even having to manage ministry without her worried him.

Mary had noticed that the numbers attending church indeed dropped dramatically, but Ritchie had explained that this was normal since so many of them were students who went home for the vacation. She scarcely noticed that several people were avoiding her and that fewer people were asking for her to pray with them. In fact, she took it on herself to start talking with the people who had been prayed for as they recovered on the carpet. Previously they had just been left to return to their seats on their own.

On the Sunday in late October when the clocks were put back one hour, there were 28 people in the hall for the morning service; a year previously there had been over 200. The realization that something was seriously wrong struck Mary with the force of a door slammed shut in her face. It was followed by a sense of panic because she felt incapable of doing anything about it. Why were people not coming? Even two of the stewards who helped greet people before church and tidy up afterwards were missing. Mary busied herself with their jobs, partly to take her mind off the worrying thought about falling attendances. What she didn't hear were the voices of complaint afterwards: "*She's even doing the greeting now!*" and "*She's pestering people after they get prayed for,*" and even "*If she doesn't leave, everyone else will. She's bringing the Fellowship down.*"

Mary had learned some years ago that the price paid by people who take control is the blame when things go wrong. Mary had become an irritant to several leaders within the church, who had previously found Richie a fairly malleable and easy-going person who would usually do their bidding. His marriage to Mary had given him real self-belief and confidence, and not a little obstinacy. Now they found it much harder to get their way, but falling numbers had given them an opportunity to respond.

"It falls to me to speak about the elephant in the room, Richie," started old Brian Cannon. "We spoke about this two meetings ago, but nothing was done about it. I like Mary and I have nothing against her personally, but attendances are falling because of her."

Richie was suddenly angry. In marrying Mary, he thought that he had created a kind of cozy nest for himself, in which he felt protected and safe. He resented these people who were attacking him, and his reaction was to retreat. He said very little at the meeting, and went home without talking socially with the deacons afterwards as he usually did.

Mary could tell he was upset. She knew that a head-on approach would fail, so she waited until he was ready to speak.

"They're blaming you for the fall in numbers attending," he said, finally over dinner two days later. "They say that you're doing too much and it doesn't look good or feel right."

"That's ridiculous! I'm only doing more because people aren't turning up, or they don't do it properly. Brian Cannon always had it in for you anyway. I heard that he was on the search committee and he didn't want you as pastor. Plus, his wife complained about me at work once – said she had been promised a full pay-out on her car, but the accident was her fault and she had a big excess."

Mary's words washed over Richie without much effect. She was reacting, he observed, in the way she usually did when she felt attacked: she put the blame on others. He heard little of what she said, as he was deep in thought. Mary, for her part, felt very alone. Richie seemed to be retreating into his thoughts. With little response from her husband, she felt increasingly isolated and alone, which in turn made her feel even more vulnerable and stressed.

The next day, as she was getting ready to go out to work, she announced to Richie: "I've decided it would be best for me to pull out of ministry altogether at the Fellowship. It seems that I'm the problem, so I'll withdraw. Then they'll have no one to blame but themselves. They'll see." With that, she stomped off to work.

Mary kept her word about withdrawing from ministry. She sat towards the front of the hall and, once the main part of the service was over, slipped out as unobtrusively as she could. As the months went by, slowly numbers attending church crept up towards 50. Richie emerged from his shell a little, but he didn't speak with Mary about the problems in the church. Early in the New Year he told her that he had been invited to join the pastoral team of an independent church a few miles away.

"Take it!" Mary urged him, immediately.

"Well, I really need to pray about it…"

"Sometimes you don't see an answer to prayer when it's staring you in the face!"

It was Mary's certainty and decisiveness linked to a strong desire to take the initiative – any initiative – that made up Ritchie's mind and he left the church a few weeks later.

From the start Mary was suspicious of the leaders in the new church – the Fellowship of Christ – especially Pastor Melvyn. Richie's new role with young people felt like a demotion to her, and she resented the lower profile she had. She suspected that

Melvyn was trying to exclude her from ministry: "He'll have been in contact with that Brian Cannon from *New Life* – he knows everyone." It was only a matter of four months before Mary decided to stop going to church altogether.

Richie observed her growing detachment with frustration, but he was powerless to do or say anything to make her change her mind. Occasionally over the months that followed he overheard her on the phone, sympathizing with one of the Fellowship troublemakers over an issue that he knew was none of her business, or discussing the failings of Pastor Melvyn with one of his critics. But usually she was alone; when he was at home she often found a reason to go to the spare room, where she said she needed to work on her laptop computer.

Martha opened her home to [Jesus]. She had a sister called Mary, who sat at the Lord's feet listening to what he said. But Martha was distracted by all the preparations that had to be made. She came to him and asked, "Lord, don't you care that my sister has left me to do the work by myself? Tell her to help me!"

"Martha, Martha," the Lord answered, "you are worried and upset about many things, but few things are needed – or indeed only one. Mary has chosen what is better..."
Luke 10:38b–42

They lived effectively separate lives over the next four years. Sometimes she would look at Ritchie and feel pity for him as she found him slightly pathetic, with his grand ideas and faltering manner of getting things done. Now and again Mary thought about divorce, but the notion of leaving their large house and having to make do with a small flat, and fear of what all her friends would say pushed the idea to the back of her mind again. She had thought about starting a family, but with church no longer playing a part in her life, her work was more important to her. She was promoted twice during those four years to a junior management position overseeing three groups of twenty telephone sales people. She was also now earning somewhat more than Ritchie.

Some eight months into her new job, she was instructed by Sandra, her supervisor to conduct an exercise in which she would ask for feedback on her own performance from her teams. Initially she had agreed to do it happily, knowing as she did that others at her job level had done it. She certainly didn't want to appear frightened or weak; besides, she felt well able to deal with people in her tear. But soon she was anxious about it, because she knew that some of the people under her resented the promotion she had received and she had always found them difficult to deal with and even to talk to. As she handed out the forms, she felt as if she was distributing weapons for them to shoot her with.

It was worse than she had imagined. Four thought that she was a 'control freak'. Two wrote that she rode roughshod over their needs and feelings. Most thought that she was getting the job done, but nearly half indicated that their team was 'inefficient'. As she read each anonymous form, she felt increasingly sick. The idea that they thought like this about her! How two-faced could they be? Four wrote that she often didn't say what she thought or felt.

She went home that evening and said little to Ritchie. When he went out for a meeting, she sat drinking red wine and cried. She loathed the feeling of powerlessness that she had. She hated the way that the people in her team could say those things without any responsibility or fear of retribution. She detested the way her line manager had obliged her to do this horrible feedback thing – it was bound to end like this: they envied her and indeed had never given her a chance to prove what she could do.

Gradually the tears subsided. She thought about herself and the way that when she allowed her feelings to surface, they did so with a mad uncontrolled rush, like a dam bursting overwhelming her with feelings that she could little understand, never mind control. Then Ritchie came in, fresh from his meeting.

"Hey," she said as brightly as she could. "How did the meeting go?" But he could easily see that she had been crying.

"Fine," he replied. "They're pretty happy with the way things are working out. But what's the matter? Are you upset?"

"No, no it's fine. It's a silly thing… it's really not worth talking about and I'm fine now. Are you ready for bed?"

Ten days later she had a hospital appointment with a gynecologist. Most of the other women were with their husbands and partners and initially she felt independent as she sat alone. Her appointment time passed and then a further 15 minutes went by. She started to wonder if she should have told Ritchie why she was coming. Finally a nurse approached her. "I'm sorry, Dr. Haqib is running late. There's been a bit of an emergency. You can wait and he'll see you probably in an hour or so, or you can make another appointment."

"I'll reschedule; that's fine." She got up.

"What?" the nurse replied.

Not far inside, Mary tutted to herself: *they can't deal with problems and keep appointments and the nurses don't understand English.* "I'll make a new appointment," she explained.

When she got home Ritchie had prepared dinner and as they sat eating she broached the subject. "I need to make an appointment with the doctor," she began.

"Oh, are you not feeling OK?"

"No, no, it's a woman's thing. We've been married five years now and I've not got pregnant. Sometimes I have months between periods. I'm going to see the specialist next month."

"Oh, OK." Ritchie looked amazed; they had never discussed having children and he had no idea that she had been trying to do so. He needed time to think it through: did he want to become a father? Was he ready? They were hardly the closest couple; she didn't come to church and they didn't talk about faith things any more.

Mary looked at him as he sat thinking and wondered whether he was thinking about accompanying her. He seemed to be lost in his thoughts. But she wasn't sure that she wanted him to be with her if the specialist told her she couldn't have children.

She went on her own to the hospital a few weeks later; neither of them had mentioned it again. She arrived half an hour early and went to the cafeteria. She half recognized the girl wiping the tables, but was nevertheless surprised when she approached Mary confidently. "Hey, Mary isn't it?" Mary smiled warily. "Sarah – from the Fellowship." Mary remembered the girl who ran the counseling service. It was strange that such a beautiful girl was wiping tables in a hospital canteen.

"I'm so sorry, I er…"

"Can I join you? I'm actually meant to be on my break." Mary liked the way Sarah seemed to be independent and different. She recalled that she had been married to a criminal.

The two of them chatted lightly for a quarter of an hour, avoiding the subjects of the Fellowship and Mary's reason for being at the hospital. Mary warmed to Sarah – she seemed to be genuinely interested in her. As she got up, she bit the bullet: "Look, I've got to go, but can we meet up some time and talk some more? I'd really like that." She wrote her mobile number on a paper napkin and smiled at Sarah. "Please, give me a ring. Let's do a girls' night out!"

Mary endured the intimate examinations with as much grace as she could muster. After around an hour Dr. Haqib explained that he would send a report to Mary's GP once he had gathered together all his findings. "You might want to take your husband along with you," he concluded. She nodded, resentfully. She would think about that.

Ten days later after work she saw her GP, whom she hardly knew: she had been to see her twice in ten years. She asked a few superficial questions about her work and how Ritchie was and then her face was set fairly grimly. Mary knew what she was going to say. "Dr. Haqib is quite clear. Both your tubes are blocked and you have virtually no chance of becoming pregnant. In fact he says here you have no chance whatsoever."

As she heard the doctor's words Mary was overcome with a strange sensation of dullness, almost as if her body were not hers. Then she had a thought: *Why am I not upset about this?*

"I'm sorry, Mary. I'm sorry it's not good news. Were you prepared for this?"

She thought to herself: *What could ever prepare me for such news?*

"Yes, I was." She looked at the doctor grimly and nodded. She got up, shook her hand and left. As she left the surgery, her phoned buzzed – a text message from Sarah: *Busy? I'm at the George and I'm bored.*

Instead of going home, Mary drove out to the King George pub overlooking the river. Mary talked generally about her work, avoiding mentioning the feedback exercise. She eventually spoke about why she had stopped attending the Fellowship of Christ.

"I had no idea, Mary," Sarah responded with genuine sympathy. "I actually thought you were going somewhere else. I think most people think that."

There was a silence, after which Mary explained about her feelings after the feedback exercise.

"Have you heard of Anais Nin?" Sarah asked. Mary shook her head.

"That's the right answer! Pastors' wives mustn't admit to having heard of her. She was a scandalous French woman who went to America and committed bigamy and wrote sexy stuff that nice people don't read. She knew just about everybody who was famous – actors and painters and authors... I love her stuff. Anyway she once wrote: *We don't see things as they are. We see them as we are.* I think that's really deep."

Mary looked at Sarah as she thought about what she had said. "Meaning that I am upset about this feedback thing because of who I am? Not because of what they said?"

"Something like that," Sarah responded. "But also, what they wrote down is more about them than it is about you." A wave of affection for Sarah wafted over Mary, as a child loves a doctor who takes away his earache.

"Don't you think than when people criticize you and complain about you, they reveal their own weaknesses?" Sarah explained and Mary nodded strongly, but she had never thought it.

"So... when they're complaining about my being too controlling, the truth is, that's what they're like themselves?"

"Well, maybe it's more what they'd **like** to be like!" Sarah laughed.

"What was that quote again?" asked Mary.

"We don't see things as they are. We see them as we are."

There was a silence. Mary sensed a thick fog clearing before her and inside she was smiling.

"But it also means," Sarah went on, "that it's really important to know yourself, because then you'll better understand why people get at you and why **you** see things the way you do."

When she got home, she had almost forgotten what the doctor had told her. For a moment she was surprised at herself, at the fact that she had not been more concerned.

"Sorry I'm late..." she began.

"You were working late..." Ritchie said, thinking about something else.

"No, I went for a drink with Sarah from the Fellowship."

"Oh?"

Mary was unperturbed. It clearly didn't seem odd to Ritchie that she should meet up with Sarah. "She gave me a great quote: *We don't see things as they are. We see them as we are.*" Ritchie was serving the dinner and had not taken in what she had said.

"Never mind," she thought to herself.

When she went in to work the next day she immediately took out the pile of responses from her teams and began reading them. Suddenly it seemed to her that they were differently-sized packages of evidence she had about her staff, information that could be useful. How foolish she had been, she reflected, to take their silly comments personally!

Her phone buzzed on the desk: a text from Sarah. *Always listen to your heart.* She wondered what she meant. It sounded like a clever saying, but did it have any meaning? She went back to her work reading the feedback forms. She noticed how some of them had very poor spelling; one girl had spelt her name "Mery". Her phone buzzed again. It was another text from Mary. Maybe this time there would be an explanation. "Error message: incomplete SMS." And then the message: *Always listen to your heart. It's there you'll know the truth.*

Mary huffed, lost in thought. What did she mean about listening to her heart? She was a little annoyed that her focus had been disturbed; she had been enjoying re-reading the feedbacks as bits of ammunition she could use at a later stage but now she was intrigued about this listening to your heart thing.

The phone rang. "Hey, sorry about that, Mary. I'm on a train and it went into a tunnel just as I was sending the text, so only a bit of it went, first time. You got it now?"

"Yes, yes, I've got it... Not too sure what it means though. I'll need to think about it."

"Yeah – and maybe pray about it too?"

Mary was annoyed, as if Sarah was trying to be clever at her expense.

"Sorry, Sarah, I need to go. Got someone with me just now."

"Oh, sorry, yes of course. You're at work. See you."

Always listen to your heart. It's there you'll know the truth. The message hung around her consciousness for days and then weeks. It was like a little wound on her finger: every now and then something would happen or someone would say something to make her remember it again. Finally she and Ritchie were sitting on opposite sides of the living room, he reading a book, she internet-surfing on her laptop.

"I got a message from Sarah that's been nagging me for weeks," she said. Ritchie looked up from his book. "*Always listen to your heart. It's there you'll know the truth.* What d'you think that means?"

Ritchie had his usual reflective look as he thought about it. "Knowing Sarah, what I would imagine she means is that you need to be in touch with your feelings. It's a bit like that Enneagram stuff that Graham McCreadie's into these days."

"Who's that?" she asked.

"Baptist church pastor. He's into that stuff."

Ritchie seemed to be dismissive, but if anything that encouraged Mary to go further.

"D'you think I need to be more in touch with my heart?"

"I wouldn't know about that..." he responded, feeling a little awkward because he had been put on the spot. Mary sensed again the distance between them and was surprised both by their lack of communication and the fact that she accepted it as normal.

As a child she had thrived on refusing to give in to her feelings; now she was wondering what would happen if she really felt them rather than denied them. When she told Sarah that she had a feeling that her heart was like a secret garden to which she had discovered the key, Sarah's response was: *And it's there that God's growing the fruit of his Spirit.* Mary smiled at the beauty of the idea.

They were indeed like fruit, these feelings inside her – feelings of love and joy, peace and forgiveness. Over the months that followed she spent difficult hours opening that secret garden gate to explore inside. Sometimes she was annoyed or upset at what she found – her anger and her pride, for instance. But slowly she grew confident through increasing familiarity with what lay there.

On her birthday she received a text message from Sarah: *Happy birthday ol'gal. But remember it ain't you that grows the fruit. It's God.*

Mary smiled wryly. She knew she had unfinished business with Him.

Spiritual Exercises for 8s

1   When Mary was a child "a sense of independence and being in control of things thrilled her..." If this is true of your childhood, can you pinpoint what exactly excited you about independence and control? What did it feel like when these things were taken away from you?

2   "She was gripped by the fabulous feeling of being a channel through which God could bless people." Mary seems to have blessed many people by praying for them. Was she changed and blessed? Did she grow? Why/why not?

3   Many 8s find, like Mary, that it is difficult to allow feelings of weakness, hurt and grief to come to the surface. One way of doing so is to reflect on what makes you angry, because anger often covers a weakness. Try this as a reflective exercise: recall one recent episode when you became angry (whether you showed it or not). Is there a weakness you were hiding?

4   Make a list of the friends you see most frequently. Which (if any) of them can you talk with openly about your deeper feelings and thoughts? What does it feel like when you do this? Can you develop more friendships like this?

5   Perhaps it was for 8s that someone once pointed out that we are human beings, not human doings. Try to be less of a Martha for a day, stepping back and allowing others to take action and make decisions. What does it feel like? How do you think it feels for the people around you?

6   If you have discovered the "secret garden" Mary learned about, are there feelings which you could share safely for the first time with someone?

7   The apostle Paul realized that it was through his weaknesses that God could show his strength (**2 Corinthians 12:9**). What are the weaknesses in you which

God could use? Pray about this and for the courage to stay weak, rather than to yearn for strength.

Sarah's Story: Type 4

My God, my God, why have you forsaken me?
Why are you so far from saving me,
so far from my cries of anguish?
My God, I cry out by day, but you do not answer,
by night, but I find no rest...
But I am a worm and not a man,
scorned by everyone, despised by the people.
Psalm 22:1–8

Sarah noticed Michael chatting with Dion, the praise band drummer after the service. She looked at him for a long time. She sensed his need for her so powerfully that it was as if someone had winded her slightly. She approached the two of them and greeted Michael warmly. It was slightly frustrating for Sarah that Dion didn't seem to sense Michael's deeper feelings at all, but over the years she had come to realize that she had a special talent for this which most others lacked – an antenna, as it were, for people's feelings and needs.

She looked at Dion and tried to smile. "Your wife is waiting in the car," she heard herself saying, but immediately she wondered why she had said it. At least it meant that she was left alone with Michael.

She looked at Michael, very aware that he found her attractive. "It would be good for us to talk, you know, Michael, if you want. I've done my "Basics of Counseling" course and I could do with some practice... Maybe we could meet for coffee sometime in the church lounge?" The way he replied, you would almost have thought she had invited him out on a date. Nevertheless Sarah was very happy about being able to help him sort himself out.

Nearly two years previously she had left the quiet and conservative Anglican church that she had once loved. She had been on

Vicar Edgar's wavelength; he had helped her through the tough times when Kenny had been arrested and then convicted of fraud; he had agreed with her on some changes to the communion liturgy which made it more reflective and somehow profound: a pause with music here, a sung psalm there... But there were people in the church whom she disliked and who were probably jealous of her. So, when a neighbor of hers had asked her for a lift to the Fellowship, it had given her an excuse to try somewhere different. Almost immediately she felt at home; people appreciated her and she sensed she could be so useful in this very different church. She had also received immediate support when she volunteered to undertake counseling training at a local college; they even part-funded her, with the agreement that once she had qualified she would help set up a counseling service in the church.

She hadn't studied since leaving school four years previously and she had found school very difficult. Not that Sarah was unintelligent; rather she was just not interested in learning about math or biology or computing. She enjoyed art, but the art teacher wanted her to draw fruit when she wanted to draw portraits, and pieces of work which she felt very happy with seemed to get lower marks than ones she dashed off in a few minutes with little effort. So she left school aged 17, and after a few short-term jobs managed to find work at the hospital working in the canteen.

All through school Sarah had felt 'outside the box'. Once, in a moment of profound and painful insight, she had imagined herself playing an entirely different game from everyone else, even those friends who spoke to her: it was like she was playing snooker when they were playing football. Some of the children spoke behind her back about her being "snobby" or "proud", neither of which was true, but she did sometimes feel that she was experiencing life somehow differently from everyone else. If the teacher was telling a moving story, for instance, she would feel tears rising to her eyes and clouding her vision, when the other children in her class seemed to be either indifferent or even amused.

Things took a turn for the worse when, aged nine, she had been chosen to be photographed for the school's publicity booklet. It was a modest but semi-private school which drew in children from a fairly wide area and every three or four years the school's governors revamped the publicity booklet. The photographer was the mother of one of the children in second form, and she spent a whole day photographing her around the school, as the "face of St Agnes's". As a result, virtually all the children in the school knew that Sarah had been picked out as special. Many of the older girls with ambitions for the role simply stopped even noticing her. Some of the boys started pushing up their noses when she came near, taunting her with silly names like "Sexy Sarah". She hadn't the faintest idea what they meant and she had no intention of trying to find out.

When the booklets appeared and Sarah's golden hair adorned a thousand copies of the glossy brochure, even some of the teachers seemed to stonewall her. In truth, Sarah didn't understand the fuss about her looks: she knew she was very pretty but she didn't care very much. Some days she hated having to brush her hair for twenty minutes, but she did it to keep her mother happy.

Home life was sometimes quite strained. One day, both her mother and father had been very upset when Sarah had told them that she had found out what had happened at the time of her birth.

"What do you mean, Sweetie?" asked her mother, sitting opposite her father near the fireside.

"They made a mistake at the hospital." Why were they so dense? Why could they not realize what she was saying? Or were they going to deny it?

"What mistake, Sweetie?" asked her mother.

"Jennifer Hogg says the same thing."

"Darling, who's Jennifer Hogg?"

"In my class. Her birthday's the day after mine."

By now her father was looking away from the television and apparently thinking, but not looking at Sarah. "But what mistake, Sarah?" he asked.

"We got mixed up."

Suddenly, with some horror, Sarah's mother realized what she was saying. "You mean you think they swapped you and Jennifer as babies?"

Sarah nodded, tears filling her eyes.

"But you were born in Swansea, sweetheart, and unless this Jennifer in your class was born there, then I'm quite sure it can't possibly have happened."

Sarah knew that they would deny it. She turned on her heels and went to her room.

As an adolescent Sarah became aware of whole ranges of experience that gave her even wider and stronger feelings: a woman holding a baby close and tight made her feel tenderly maternal; a child sitting on his own while others played football prompted empathy; an old couple walking slowly to the shops made her feel sad; the young man outside the supermarket selling the *Big Issue* caused feelings of anger at the social injustice that meant that some people were wealthy and others poor… It was as if her heart was a radio with a capacity to receive signals from far and wide, so each day she could go through dozens of powerful feelings and it was these feelings which made her feel alive.

She first noticed Kenny on the very day that he started in the same school, when they were 14. They were in the same class. For several weeks he didn't wear a uniform; when she asked him why not, it turned out that his parents were waiting for a grant from the parish council. The poorer children in the school were usually reluctant to admit they got parish help, so immediately

Sarah was taken with Kenny's honesty. She could well imagine his modest home, with bare floorboards and threadbare curtains. Suddenly she felt guilty at her own family's wealth and wondered if Kenny would like a ride in her father's Lexus – she would ask him one day.

What she loathed at school were the leering looks she got from boys, even some of the ones two and three years older than her. It made them look like animals when they stared like that at the shapeliness of her body. She tried tying her hair back like a nun, but then she felt her face was very exposed. She asked several times for a larger, baggy blouse but her mother insisted on buying the shaped and tailored blouses that were three times the price of the simple ones. She even tried wearing woolen stockings like the ones that her gran wore, but her teacher told her they were not permitted in the school's uniform policy.

The sense of her own uniqueness might have made someone else very lonely, but Sarah thrived on it. In fact she hated the way that school made her similar in some ways to others; she liked standing out or being in the sidelines. And the feelings she had were like a drug that made her feel real – she was a buzzing cauldron of intense sensations, together with memories that could themselves provoke sadness, or a feeling of tragedy – usually a 'down' emotion of some kind.

As she neared her sixteenth birthday (which she knew would bring something important and deep) she also consciously realized for the first time that by helping someone she could put her powerful feelings on hold – at least for a while. Kenny was the first candidate. He was amazed when she invited him to tea at her house on the following Saturday (she would sort it with her mother that evening) but he accepted gladly and Sarah felt she had done something heroic. None of her classmates talked about Kenny in terms other than disdain; they all knew he was poor and rumor had it that his father had served time in prison.

Her mother was delighted that at last her beautiful daughter had shown signs of interest in a boy. Their only child, she had once or twice fantasized about the wedding they would have for her – a wedding that would be the talk of the neighborhood. For some reason she was quite sure that Sarah would meet the son of a wealthy landowner or even a minor royal when she went to university, and so the wedding would be quite a society affair, but she kept these thoughts to herself. She looked forward to Saturday evening and to meeting Kenneth.

He was half an hour late turning up. It was with horror that Sarah's mother opened the door for him. "Sorry, I couldn't see the house numbers up the drives and I got bitten by a dog at number seven." And with that he walked in, pushing past her as if he was entering a pub. His trousers were creased and his shirt was at least two sizes too big for him. She led him into the lounge, hardly able to speak and had him sit on one of the leather armchairs, but he insisted on sitting straddling the arm. Then she scurried upstairs and knocked on her daughter's bedroom door. She was crying.

"What's the matter?" she asked, hurrying over to Sarah.

"I knew he wouldn't come…" she blurted out, pitifully.

"He's here."

"What? Really? Kenny's here?!" She stopped crying and wiped her face.

"Just wash your face, Sweetie, and come down to your guest." Her mother decided that she would try to make the best of it. Clearly, she determined, this would be the first and last time that Kenneth would be in the house.

If it hadn't been so excruciating, the tea invitation would have been hilarious. Kenny revealed that they didn't have a table in their house; he didn't know what a scone was; he only ever drank Coke, never tea or coffee; he seemed to be genuinely at a loss when they revealed that they didn't have any brown sauce to accompany the scrambled eggs.

The torture looked like ending around seven o'clock when

Kenny announced that he would have to leave. Sarah's father noted that it was scarcely an hour since he had arrived, but the sooner he was off the premises, the less likely it was that anything would get stolen. He had by now realized that this was Kenny Smith. Their family, sometimes known as Roma Smith, was well-known to the police and figured in reports from the courts on a regular basis. He would explain this to Sarah when she returned from showing Kenny to the bus stop and that would be the end of that.

Sarah had never held a boy's hand before but she pretended that it was the most natural thing in the world as they walked airily down the road towards the station where the bus stop was. For all the reasons that horrified her mother, Sarah was delighted: he was so different! And he didn't seem to be afraid to stand out. She knew the stories about his family's being 'gypsies' but this just added to the exotic excitement of dating him. His swarthy and rough looks made him look like Heathcliff, she decided. He didn't speak as they neared the station and she realized that she loved this mysterious side of him. He didn't seem to be surprised when she suggested that they walk on the next stop.

When he pulled her off the pavement and towards the thin line of trees skirting the field, she was taken by surprise to begin with, but quickly she imagined that her Heathcliff was overcome with passion for his Catherine. His rough arms held her tightly as he kissed her and she followed his lead, even when his tongue was in her mouth. Somehow she disliked it intensely, but at the same time she felt that it was wonderful and romantic. It lasted for two or three minutes and then, without saying a thing, they resumed their walk along the pavement. She saw him onto the bus and waved brightly as he sat down; he didn't seem to notice her. She stood and watched the bus drive away and then turned back to walk home.

Her mother was in the kitchen loading dishes into the

dishwasher when Sarah let herself into the house. She went upstairs and then up the narrow flight of stairs that led to the attic rooms. She sat in the dusty room she called the library and reflected on the evening's events. She could still taste Kenny on her tongue. So, she now had a boyfriend! She loved the way he didn't fit in at school and at her home; how out of the ordinary he seemed. She wished she could write poetry, because this would be a great subject for a poem, but try as she might, she had never succeeded in putting her feelings down in words.

To her dismay, her mother appeared at the door a few minutes later. The argument that followed was similar to many she had had with her mother: Sarah found it frustrating that her mother was limited to social niceties and keeping up appearances; her mother was appalled at Sarah's lack of judgment and her capacity to take the side of the loser! Momentarily she remembered her dream of a society wedding for her daughter and then considered the prospect of a sordidly brief event at the registry office with this scruffy gypsy and it made her angry. Her daughter would not rob her of her dream, she determined.

"I don't want him in the house again," she concluded.

"No problem," Sarah responded truculently, "we'll meet at his house."

Over the next two years or so their relationship alternated between brief bouts of intense passion and longer periods when she refused to see Kenny: she knew that he was seeing other girls and she was so jealous she couldn't bear to be with him. She got occasional glimpses of his family life from things he said: his older brother (in whose flat they would usually meet) was in trouble because he had helped out someone else and it turned out that the cigarettes had been stolen... His father was constantly getting picked on by the police, and getting blamed for 'jobs' that he couldn't possibly have done. But then Linksmoor warehouse was robbed, and Kenny's father was in trouble for it. It made the national papers and Sarah bathed in a feeling of reflected infamy.

By now she had left school and was working as a catering assistant at the hospital. The stress which the latest Smith family saga caused led directly to the marriage. Kenny was in tears at times, explaining that his father was "going down" and his mother was moving in with someone else, who had four children of his own. Their house had been "torched" for the insurance money. He couldn't stay with his brother for much longer because the cigarettes had indeed been stolen.

Sarah had had a vague belief that the Smiths were involved in petty crime, but she knew the important difference between facts and truth: it may be a fact that they did some crime, but the truth was that they had been victimized and cut off from normal society. If they had done some of the criminal things they had been accused of, it was clearly because they could find no honest way of making a living. The Roma Smiths were so infamous no one would offer them a job. Kenny himself had tried to get work at the local McDonalds, but had been turned down apparently because the manager thought Kenny would steal things.

In Sarah's kindly and caring heart, it therefore made perfect sense that she should marry Kenny to rescue him from all this. She told her mother one cold November evening when she had left Kenny's brother's flat with no heating on at all and had returned to the huge and cozy warmth of her own house. She looked at her daughter with a complete puzzlement: how could she make such a mistake? Why was she so perverse? Was she doing this to anger her parents? Her parents eventually gave in six weeks later when they realized that their opposition was only confirming Sarah in her decision. Her father, in a rare moment of ironic humor, suggested that they should send a wedding photo to Country Life magazine and name it "Beauty and the Beast".

The wedding at Grangefield Priory was a magnificent affair and Sarah swanned through the comical and pathetic aspects of it blissfully unaware of them all. Kenny, by turns amazed and puzzled, did his best to play the part expected of him while his father sat gloomily looking on attached to an even gloomier prison warden by a rather short chain.

The flat Sarah's parents bought for them above the estate agents' office was her delight. It didn't matter to her that their names, rather than hers, were on the title deeds. Kenny was away once or twice a week with his work as a lorry-driver's mate, but she loved the way the flat had become their haven, as if Catherine and Heathcliff had had a happy ending after all. When he was home, Kenny didn't speak a great deal, but Sarah was happy with that and he seemed to be content enough to listen to her talking. Her parents didn't visit.

It lasted just under five months. A policewoman came to visit Sarah one evening and spent three hours with her explaining the whole sad story. Kenny and his brother had been involved in illegal sales of cars for some five years, taking badly-damaged cars and having them welded back together. A man in Scotland had died in an accident caused by faulty welding and the trail led back to Kenny himself. The policewoman explained that he had never had a job as a lorry-driver's mate; he had been involved in crime. They thought he had at least a quarter of a million pounds stashed away, but they couldn't for the time being locate it. If they did, most if not all of it would be confiscated.

Her eyes had been cruelly opened of course, but Sarah sensed the tragic in Kenny's situation no less than in her own. She wasn't angry with him for having so comprehensively duped her, because she was more than ever the heroine in her own tragedy: she had tried against all the odds to rescue Kenny and had failed. This narrative worked for her better than the alternative – that she had been wrong all along about Kenny and he had deceived her wickedly. When the lawyer phoned, she didn't ask him whether her mother had asked him to do so; she knew and she agreed to file for divorce.

A few weeks passed, during which Sarah was low and bordering on depressed. The memories of her relationship with Kenny kept flooding over her like uninvited guests. Time and again she was reminded of him – by the color of someone's hair, by a passing comment, by noticing an odd car or by a style-less pullover someone in the bus was wearing. She refused to see her parents and was too embarrassed to see friends. She dragged herself through workdays as if her body was a burden to her; she volunteered for unpopular late shifts so that she would not see so many people.

Slowly Sarah came out of her shell. She visited her parents twice – on her mother's birthday and at Christmas, but she felt distant from them. The divorce progressed steadily through its stages, but Sarah had started using her maiden name again. She had returned unopened three letters Kenny had sent from prison, where he had been on remand awaiting trial. He had pleaded guilty and was sentenced to nine months imprisonment.

The card dropped through the door like any other might do, but with her heightened sensitivity, Sarah knew that it was special the very second it landed on the doormat. She got up and walked with measured steps towards it. What was it that made her aware of its specialness? She had received several messages of condolence since Kenny's trial, as if someone had died. This card, in its creamy-yellow envelope was different. It was signed "Edgar Hoggart" and the parish stamp indicated it came from the church. There were some comforting words printed inside which she didn't read because her eyes were immediately drawn to the Bible verse printed in bold halfway down:

...in all things God works for the good of those who love him

Slightly to one side and below it was added: "Rom 8:28". Did this "Rom" have anything to do with the Roma? Presumably so; Edgar Hoggart was the parish priest and perhaps he knew.

Suddenly she was captivated by this mystery and by the beautiful thought that somehow even the mess of her life was going to work out good.

The early morning sung Eucharist she attended at the church was very moving and she learned several things she didn't know about Jesus Christ. She was particularly touched by the notion that Jesus had died instead of sinners but that he himself was innocent – an awesome tragedy. She saw the people standing receiving little wafers and taking tiny sips of wine from the bright shiny goblet and she was transfixed. Her parents, who were devout atheists, had never told her about this! She found herself crying quietly to herself at the end of the service and was surprised to feel a hand touching hers.

"May I pray for you?" asked Edgar. She nodded, and as he prayed she was filled with a warmth deep inside that she had never felt before.

"Thanks for the card. It was very kind of you. How did you know?"

"Well, I'm afraid everyone knows…"

"No, I mean how did you know what to write in the card?"

"Oh, they're lovely aren't they? I think a lot of people find them very helpful. Was there a verse or a prayer that specially spoke to you?" He was very gentle and sensitive, Sarah decided.

"About God working things out for good…" she replied.

"Oh yes…" said Edgar.

"And what does the "Rom" number mean? Is it code?"

For a few moments Edgar wondered if Sarah was slightly mentally disturbed.

"It says Rom 328," she explained.

"Oh, that's where the verse is from in the Bible: Romans, third chapter, 28th verse."

"I see." Sarah's heart sank a little, but she tried to hide it. Edgar had his hand on hers and in her vulnerable and lonely state Sarah felt its protective and affectionate meaning with profound power.

"Do you mean God is making something good happen out of Kenny getting done?"

"I think it is possible, Sarah."

The picture developed slowly in her mind's eye over the next few days: she had seen pictures of the phoenix, rising from the charred ashes of a fire and she imagined that she was that phoenix, with God lifting her out of the mess of her life. And with that reflection came the next one: that she had been fated to fail in her marriage so that she could find inner spiritual renewal. This was her destiny – sad, messy, painful, but nevertheless her destiny.

She started attending the parish church regularly; she was baptized and confirmed and went to meetings about the liturgy that Edgar held. She was by far the youngest person in the church and certainly the prettiest. Edgar enjoyed the attention from Sarah, although he found her a bit too intense. Mrs. Cooper and Mrs. Stotter noticed the amount of time that Edgar and Sarah spent in each other's company and reported it to Mrs. Cooper's brother-in-law, the bishop, who discretely initiated the moves which led to Edgar's move away to another parish.

Mrs. Cooper approached Sarah as she sipped a cup of tea after a service a few weeks after Edgar's departure.

"I had no idea you were Helen and William's daughter," she began.

At once Sarah's hackles rose. "Oh, do you know them?"

"They are bridge friends of my sister's, but we meet socially at times." Sarah noticed that Mrs. Cooper said 'times' so as to rhyme with 'dames'. "But imagine this: they didn't know you came to church with us!" There was a pause. "They didn't even know you had been baptized. Isn't that strange?"

"Not at all strange, Mrs. Cooper. I live my life; they live theirs."

"Oh my, how sad… Not quite what Jesus had in mind, is it?"

Once she had the knife in, Mrs. Cooper clearly knew how to twist it. She turned away and began talking with the curate who had taken the service. Sarah placed her cup quietly and carefully on the table, turned around and resolved to never return.

That evening, she went to the Fellowship with her neighbor, Mrs. Rogers, who had asked her for a lift as it was raining heavily. Pastor Melvyn's sermon was homely and warm, but too long and at times boring. He paid special attention to her as she left, shaking her hand warmly, with his other hand sandwiching hers in the way that he had learned recently at an evangelism conference. It certainly worked with Sarah: she smiled broadly at him and he was delighted to see so attractive a young woman starting at church. "I usually try and visit people who visit the church. May I do that some time?"

"Of course you can," she replied.

"If you could just write your address on the bottom of the sheet you got when you came in, I'll try and make it this week."

In her heart of hearts, Sarah felt special. Frequently she felt that the world was an odd place to live and that she was the only normal person in it. She thought, for instance, that many rules about car parking or even one-way streets did not apply to her; she imagined herself dancing to an entirely different tune from everyone else. When people confirmed her in this subconscious feeling about specialness by giving her extra attention, she usually responded with eagerness and sometimes even more than that – adoration, bordering on adulation. She felt an affinity for people who stalked the object of their desires, but she had never tried it herself. Moreover she had a soft spot for people in high places; authority figures and remote, hard-to-reach people were deliciously appealing to her. She had fallen for Edgar, and now Pastor Melvyn seemed to be coming onto the scene.

Pastor Melvyn had none of Edgar's refinement and class, though and when he visited two days later she was rather disappointed with him. He was safe and reliable, but on a very different wavelength from her own. She noticed the way he was looking at her and decided to try him out.

"Melvyn, I was touched by the part of your message on Sunday evening when you spoke about the Fellowship showing its love and care for the community by perhaps developing a Counseling service…"

"Yes, it's something which the elders have discussed once or twice over the past couple of years, but no one has come forward to head it up."

"Hm, well I know it's very early days yet, but I'd be really interested," Sarah explained, piercing Melvyn's weak gaze with her own. "I don't want to seem pushy…"

"No, no, not at all… I er…" Melvyn sensed that here was a pretty and valuable church member dropping – as it were – into his lap. He blinked as he momentarily imagined Sarah in his lap and he blushed slightly.

Meanwhile Sarah had had a thought: "Perhaps that's why I've been led to the Fellowship," she suggested, tentatively.

"We need to be open to what God is saying and how he is leading us," Melvyn said, piously. He was silent for a moment, gathering his thoughts and Sarah watched him as he did so. "Well, let me raise it with the elders at the next meeting, which is in about three weeks or so. Meantime why don't you pray about it and look into the practicalities – courses, times and dates, fees… we wouldn't expect you to foot the course fees bill yourself, of course."

"Oh, well, that would be very helpful. I don't earn much at the hospital. I will do that, thanks."

So it was that Sarah started studying for a two-year counseling diploma, while a small support group at the Fellowship looked into how a service could be set up. She met regularly with Pastor Melvyn, who seemed to be in awe of Sarah. She enjoyed that a great deal.

Counseling drew Sarah out of herself in a way that she was

very grateful for. Acutely conscious of a painful past with memories that still brought tears to her eyes, listening to others' life stories distracted her. As she heard her clients speaking, she sometimes read between the lines of their words and imagined other incidents in their past – the loss of a parent or a tragic illness – as she empathized with them. If she didn't like them – and she had an ability to measure people up quickly, sometimes even before they started speaking – then the imagined incidents usually reflected badly on them: they had themselves been cruel to a family pet or neglected an important duty.

Her clients in the early stages of her training frequently had the sense that she was listening, but in a way that suggested there was turmoil within her. Their words would sometimes provoke evident pain or grief, to the point that three of her clients significantly understated their stories so that they wouldn't upset her.

The support group at the Fellowship found her difficult and tetchy at times, but since Melvyn was enthralled with her, no one complained. They got on with the business of making links with local GPs and social workers, to inform them of the new service. They thought it expedient to not mention that the sole counselor was the naïve young woman who had so disastrously married Kenny Roma.

A few years later, Sarah agreed to go for a day to the "Fresh Wine" festival with Grace, who led the women's group in the Baptist church. She didn't like being in large crowds, but she had decided to go because Grace was such a warm and kindly person and she had referred several people to the counseling service at the Fellowship.

As she stood in the huge marquee tent, in the midst of 2,000 people singing a very loud and boisterous praise song, to begin with she was floating in the internal world of her feelings with which she was very familiar. But as she sensed her own safety – the profound truth that she had nothing to fear and nothing to be ashamed of – she felt as if she were unwrapping herself, like a tulip or a rose opening to the sun's brightness for the first time.

Somewhere deep in her soul she sensed a kind of blessed anonymity among those hundreds of bouncing and dancing bodies. Instead of her own uniqueness – a feeling she had had all her life – she now felt like a nameless dot in this mass of humanity, and it was a wonderful liberation. The smell of the damp ground rose and filled her nostrils; the colors of the tent and the crowd's multifarious clothing made her smile; the fabulous experience of that particular moment struck her with a force as if a wave had swallowed her up into the sea. She heard the joyful chords of the guitars and keyboard and the powerful rhythm of the drums and instead of withdrawing into herself to reflect on what she felt about it, for the first time in her adult life she was borne away with the flow, caught up in its melody and cadence and dancing unselfconsciously for joy in the presence of her God.

Spiritual Exercises for 4s

1   Listen to a piece of music that you like and, instead of asking yourself what you feel about it, try to analyze how the sound was created and put together.

2   When someone else is talking, notice how often you become aware of what you feel about what is being said and how it is expressed. Just notice this; do not try to repress or hide it.

3   Feelings of self-hatred and self-contempt are common for many 4s. Meditate and reflect on this truth: "God loves you despite your feelings about yourself." If you hear contrary voices as you reflect on this, consciously respond: "No, that is not true."

4   *"Somewhere deep in her soul she sensed a kind of blessed anonymity..."* Can you imagine what this feels like? Is there something to fear here? What?

5   When you withdraw from others' company, can you understand why? Do you feel shame? Or fear? Why?

6   Reflect on this verse from **1 John 4**: ***this is love, not that we have loved God, but that he loved us...*** Recognize that God's love for you has nothing to do with your feelings of lovability or otherwise.

7   Go for a walk and instead of allowing yourself to wallow in your own feelings and memories, deliberately try to answer the question: *"What is happening in the world all around me?"* Try to mentally list things that you see, feel and hear.

Michael's Story: Type 6

Now Thomas (also known as Didymus), one of the Twelve, was not with the disciples when Jesus came. So the other disciples told him, "We have seen the Lord!" But he said to them, "Unless I see the nail marks in his hands and put my finger where the nails were, and put my hand into his side, I will not believe."
John 20:24–25

It was painful for Michael to think about leaving the small town in the British Midlands where he was born and grew up: he lived with his parents and most of his family and friends were there; he knew the town well and had a kind of routine in his life, centered in the town. He had played for the local football club for 12 years – since he was a teenager. In the winter he loved playing darts for his local pub. Michael was a classic 'team player' who got on well with most people and his friends would be sad to see him go too. He worked for a large insurance company, mostly doing paperwork in their local office, but with some customer contact.

Two years previously he had met Emma, who was on a six-month nursing contract doing maternity cover. Towards the end of the contract they had a bit of a crisis: it looked like Emma would have to return home to Leeds, and for three weeks she had pleaded with Michael to come with her. He had been torn between his feelings for Emma – she was the first girl he had seriously thought about marrying – and his reluctance to leave home. Out of the blue she was offered a 9-month extension, and then another, which delayed the decision for Michael once again, but now she was definitely leaving, and the arguments started again six weeks before her employment would come to an end.

"Why are you so keen to stay in this run-down place? It's so boring! You even say so yourself." They had been over this ground so often she knew what his response would be.

"It's home, Emma," he would reply, "and I know it's a bit boring, but it's like a–"

"Comfortable pair of slippers," she groaned, finishing his sentence for him.

"Yes, it is. I guess I'm not like you. It's hard for me to up sticks and leave. The idea of going somewhere else and getting a new job and trying to make new friends – all that really makes me scared."

"Well, if you really prefer this crummy little place to me, then it doesn't say very much for us, does it?" By now she was nearly in tears, but Michael felt she was also exaggerating. Besides, she could surely get a job nearer than Leeds, somewhere close enough to be able to commute each day.

These arguments unsettled Michael in a way that nothing else could. They seemed somehow to reach deep into his guts and twist them around, making him anxious and fearful. While Emma seemed to be so clear in her own mind while they argued, he just became increasingly upset. And then, when he contemplated the prospect of life without Emma, he was thoroughly terrified: what would he do without her?

Big decisions, for Michael, were torture. It wasn't that he was stuck for advice – he had lots of friends to whom he turned at times like this, but their opinions differed and he found it nearly impossible to decide who was right and who was wrong. His mother had urged him to "follow his heart" and go with Emma, while his father said very little about it, but clearly wanted Michael to stay. Most of his friends were against a move; his best friend from school told him that he might regret it for a long time if he let Emma go. How could he decide?

Michael's faith had long been a source of security for him. The familiar hymns and songs, the ritual of communion and the minister's teaching were like a grounding or foundation to his life. It wasn't that he got all his answers this way – in fact sometimes he got more questions than answers, but at least he felt that there was something really secure and reliable in his life. He went to see his minister after a particularly upsetting fight with Emma. His answer was sadly predictable: "I think you need to pray about it and decide what your own mind is, Michael. I can't tell you what to do. And y'know, God doesn't overrule our free will; he uses it!"

Michael had drifted in his faith in the past five years. He found that although it was good to feel that God was close at hand and even right there with him in moments of crisis, in the quietness of prayer his mind filled with all manner of questions, problems and possible scenarios – some of them ridiculously unlikely, like winning a million pounds on his premium bonds: then, neither of them would have to work and he could buy a big fancy house half a mile from his parents.

Michael's father Tom was also his most trusted friend, so when he asked him along to an adult baptism at the church Fellowship where his brother, Michael's uncle Melvyn, was pastor he accepted. His father had stopped going to church some years ago, citing a disagreement with the then minister, so this was also an opportunity to see if his father would get back into the churchgoing habit. Melvyn was very passionate and fervent, and Tom often called the fellowship he pastored "a bit over the top." There was often shouting and screaming during worship, and at the monthly healing meetings people cried out and often people claimed to be healed of long-standing illnesses. If Emma had known that he was going along, she would have been angry: she worked with a nurse who had a very bad experience there: she had been told that she "had a demon" inside her when in fact it was a haunting memory of childhood abuse.

But on the Sunday morning after his unhelpful interview with the minister, and with the coincidence of his father's invitation (it was a workmate of his who was being baptized), the controversial "Fellowship of Christ" meeting in a local secondary school seemed to Michael like a genuine answer to prayer – even though he hadn't actually prayed.

From the first contact Michael was thrilled to be there. The young lady on the door was Sarah, whom he remembered from school. Married at 19, her husband had become involved in illegal car sales and was sent to prison for a year. She had divorced him, returned home and, as the locals said, "got God." She was just as good-looking as Michael remembered and it excited him that someone as cool as Sarah should be welcoming him to church. The older man alongside her handing out notice-sheets had a strong handshake and a firm gaze that Michael took note of. It was noisy and relaxed in the school foyer, but from this first encounter Michael sensed that the people around him had an assurance about their faith that he didn't see a lot in his own church.

The praise band in the corner were up and running in antici-pation. Michael was growing more and more excited about the place: why had he never been here before? Then the drums clattered powerfully and a guitar played out the first notes of a familiar hymn, *Blessed Assurance*. Michael was transfixed. Ninety minutes passed as if in a moment. At the end of the service, he wanted to stay behind and maybe catch up with Sarah, but his father was keen to leave so he left with him.

"Well, what did you think?" he asked Tom as they walked out of the school gates.

"Awful lot of fuss about not a lot, I'd say," Tom replied. "People can believe what they want I reckon, but what's the big deal about getting soaked in a paddling pool just to tell everyone?"

Michael was silent. For one thing, he knew that when his father was in this 'mind-made-up' mood, there was no point disagreeing with him, since he just got more annoyed and critical. For another, Michael sensed that in this fellowship he had found what he had for years unknowingly been looking for:

a church that was lively, fun and where people really believed what they said they believed.

He didn't tell Emma that he had been to the Fellowship of Christ. That afternoon they drove the thirty miles into Birmingham and did some shopping, then went bowling and out for dinner at a restaurant popular with young and fairly affluent couples.

"Do you think we will get married, Mike?" asked Emma, quite suddenly. It was something she had asked several times before and he had given the same answer, "I don't know." It felt to Michael like a negative switch suddenly switched on inside Emma's mind and her face developed that strong, fixed and hard expression that scared him somewhat.

"Well, do you want to get married? I mean, to anyone at all?" Now she was looking sarcastic and angry and Michael panicked. "Well, I don't know!" he responded. When she was angry like this, he found it even harder than usual to think straight. But at least she didn't go on: instead she became quiet and slightly distant, as if she was partly absent from him. The rest of the evening was marked by staccato conversation and long silences, but Emma didn't ask him again about marriage, or even leaving home in order to be with her.

The truth was, Emma had by now decided that her relationship with Michael was finished. He was too weak for her, she thought. They had been very good friends at the start of her time at the hospital, when she had known noone in this small town. He was easy to be with, good-looking and he usually agreed to do what she wanted to do. But now his indecision and weakness irritated her. She needed someone stronger. She also had ambitions that Michael would probably find too demanding, she concluded. She was a little ashamed to be able to cut herself off from Michael so easily, not least because he had been so loyal to her – even after the hen-night episode a year previously, when she had slept with an ex-boyfriend. Michael's readiness to forgive humbled her. (For Michael's part, the thought of losing Emma at that time had been unthinkable; the forgiveness was more out of dread of losing her.)

As the next couple of weeks passed by he was persuaded that God was leading him into a deeper and more muscular faith. The certainties which he was lapping up at the Sunday and midweek fellowship meetings were a powerful antidote to his doubts and he was feeling stronger almost daily. His prayer life was transformed; instead of weak and rambling requests he found himself declaiming strong prayers about Emma's salvation and being "freed from the power of the evil one." It didn't trouble him that his newfound religion wasn't mature or deep: it was the easy form of conviction that comes from excluding others' points of view and the possibility of being wrong. This was what he needed at the moment; it worked for him. Actually, Michael loved being whipped up into fervent zeal during the services because it gave him security. If he had been able to reflect honestly on himself, Michael would have seen that his faith arose more from fear than from love of God.

Secretly he also had fantasies about dating Sarah, in which he told himself that she would share his faith in a way that Emma never had. So, for Michael also, the relationship with Emma was all but over, but the idea of telling her was terrifying.

Three weeks after his first visit to the Fellowship, Sarah edged towards him as he chatted with a praise band drummer after the service and greeted him warmly.

"Hey, Michael, good to see you again. You're looking really smart: that jacket really suits you!"

"Hi, Sarah!" was all Michael could stammer out, embarrassed to be approached by Sarah in front of someone else. Now they would both see how awkward he was, he thought to himself. Sarah smiled at the drummer and said in a confidential tone, "Your wife is waiting in the car…" The drummer hastened away, waving at Sarah and Michael as he left the room.

"I heard about Emma and you... It would be good for us to talk, you know, Michael, if you want. I've done my "Basics of Counseling" course and I could do with some practice... Maybe we could meet for coffee sometime in the church lounge? I'll need to make sure it's free."

Michael could hardly believe his ears: he had found such strength in this fellowship, it was like his faith had been renewed and now here was the very lovely Sarah offering to give him some advice and support! He noticed the way her lips shaped over her teeth when she smiled and he was slightly mesmerized. God seemed to be pouring out blessings on him by the bucketload.

"That would be really good," he said, smiling just a little bit too broadly: then he reminded himself that they were after all planning to discuss his problems rather than meet for a romantic tête-à-tête.

Two days later, when Emma went to the hospital canteen for lunch, Sarah spoke to her for the first time in over a year. "Hi, Emma," she began, with her usual disarming warmth. "Could you tell Michael that the church lounge is free at 6 o'clock tomorrow as we planned?" Emma had no idea what to say, and just nodded. Who was this person who seemed to know her and Michael so well? And what were the two of them going to do in the church lounge?

That evening, Michael felt the full brunt of Emma's anger when they met in the pub. It was the one trait in her which he simply didn't know how to handle. "What's so special about Sarah that you need her to be your counselor? And doesn't she go to that loopy church? Is that where you're going to meet?"

Michael couldn't reply. Whenever he sensed her anger, his words wouldn't come out properly, and in his mind he panicked. He felt slightly guilty about meeting up with Sarah, but he looked mortified.

"I always thought that I could rely on you, Michael," Emma

complained. "Now I just don't know what's got into you: you're stubborn and secretive..." And then she sensed her moment: "I've been hoping – maybe you might call it praying – for a clear answer and I think I've got it now: I can see that you just don't live the way I do. You've got no ambitions. You love your pub and your football and your pals too much to get out. You'll still be in this pathetic little place when you're 65!"

Michael felt weak and vulnerable, like a child. He watched her in anxious silence as she clicked her handbag firmly shut on her lap, pushed her chair noisily back and walked away. Someone at the bar seemed to have noticed that she was walking out on him, but otherwise the hubbub continued as before. Michael finished his drink and took the empty glass to the bar. His strongest feeling now was relief: the uncertainty was over; he hadn't needed to make a decision.

"Hoi, Mickey!" It was Geoff Stripes, playing darts the other side of the pub with Ally Smith.

Michael's friends had little insight into his inner turmoil. All they saw was the ever-reliable pal who stuck with them through thick and thin. He was the guy they could tell their innermost thoughts to with total confidence that he would keep them secret. Most of them were also pleased to be asked their opinion whenever Michael had a decision to make and were flattered when he listened so intently to their advice.

He walked round the oval bar to where Geoff and Ally were standing.

"Wasn't that Emma with you just now?" Ally asked. Like Michael's other friends, Ally loathed Emma. He found her scary and detached, a bit like a boss who really has ambitions to be the top of the tree.

"Yes, she... had to go."

"And is she... going? I mean leaving town?" Geoff asked.

"Yes, she is."

"This is like pulling teeth!" responded Ally. "So tell us, are you going with her, are you splitting up? What's the gen, Mickey blue-eyes?"

"We're splitting up." He nodded and went to the bar to get another drink. "Either of you want another?" They shook their heads, as if in sync.

They played darts and drank beer until the barman shouted, for the fourth time, "Gentlemen, please! I shall lose my license!" Then they left. Michael went home and straight to bed.

Therefore I tell you, do not worry about your life, what you will eat or drink; or about your body, what you will wear. Is not life more than food, and the body more than clothes?... Can any one of you by worrying add a single hour to your life? So do not worry, saying, "What shall we eat?" or "What shall we drink?" or "What shall we wear?"... Therefore do not worry about tomorrow, for tomorrow will worry about itself. Each day has enough trouble of its own.
Matthew 6:25–33

The next day he was as nervous as a teenager prior to his first date. He woke early and opened the big brown trunk at the foot of his bed. Hidden away at the bottom was a shiny booklet in a brown envelope titled "St Agnes School Welcomes You". He treasured it for the photograph of Sarah which adorned the front. He was looking at it when he put it down abruptly. It felt a bit weird to be looking at a photo of a primary-aged child. He slid the booklet back into the envelope and put it under a pile of disused toys and board games.

Work dragged slowly on; he frequently looked at his watch and his attention wandered from the rather dull statements he was working his way through. He tried to rehearse what he would say that evening.

"I guess I need to get myself together, Sarah." But then he didn't want to come over as weak and needy. She must get that a lot.

"Emma wasn't the right person for me." He liked that, because it left open the question: "Who is?"

"I guess I let her set the agenda for my life…" Agh, no, soft and needy again; that wouldn't do. But then again, if he wasn't needy, what was he doing going for counseling? She would think he had tricked her into seeing him. No, wait, she had invited him. Which itself was kind of odd – a counselor offering her services… Maybe… just maybe she harbored secret feelings for him! No, he would stick with that 'agenda of my life' line; it sounded good.

"I think that sometimes, out of kindness, I go along with what other people want and then I get annoyed because it's not what I want, or need." That sounded cool, suggesting both consideration and self-knowledge. It was surely fine to be so kind that you ignored your own needs. Plus, saying that again opened up the question, "Well, what do you need, Michael?" Maybe she would ask that and he would answer, "Someone like you." Yes, that was a soft kind of thing to say, but it was very romantic and Sarah was surely romantic. He became increasingly sure that Sarah had looked at him with more than a professional interest when they had spoken at church.

He didn't eat anything prior to going out. He told his mother that he was going to a restaurant. The truth was, his stomach was churning over and over and round and round; if he ate anything, he told himself, he would probably be sick.

Some people – notably several of his friends – agreed that Sarah was a "cold fish". Beautiful, yes, but in a cold and unkind way. Geoff had once said that she was like a statue. To Michael's simpler way of thinking, she was just beautiful and he was a sucker for beauty. He was fascinated by her hair, which had darkened over the years, but it was a light brown color now, with waves and small curls that caught the light in such a way that he was entranced. When she approached him as he sat in the draughty hall, she had to walk half the length of the hall from the church lounge where she held her counseling sessions. He had several seconds (which felt like two or three minutes) to take in her comely shape and that lustrous hair of hers…

"Hey, Michael, do come through. Sorry to keep you waiting…" he was about to say, "Oh, no worries," but his larynx had quite dried up. "Sometimes it's not possible to end a session on time." He had got up now and was walking next to her. Her hips brushed against his in a way that suggested they were best friends. "So sorry again. Anyway, you OK?"

Michael nodded. He cleared his throat and a sound like rasping sandpaper came out.

"Oh, hey, that sounds a bit rough. Now I don't want to catch that!" She was smiling in a way that clearly was intended to put him at his ease. It wasn't working; he was dazzled by her. "Shall I get you a glass of water?"

He managed to make a sound in response as he nodded his head. She walked through to the kitchen adjacent and he heard her running the tap. She returned with a jug of water and two glasses. Michael cleared his throat again and grimaced. He took the glass she offered him and took a large drink. He felt slightly less tense in his throat and managed to speak.

"Thanks, I needed that. No, I'm not ill. Office air: very dry."

She looked at him with those green eyes of hers and he felt himself blush; not slowly as he tended to sometimes, but rapidly, as if he were choking on food.

"It's so funny to be in this situation… we were at school together, what, 15 years ago…" Michael nodded. He knew exactly how long he had known her, but just nodded. He wanted to say that he hadn't been one of those who had called her "sexy Sarah" but the truth was he had indeed been one of them and he had a strong suspicion she would remember. Somehow it wouldn't sound right if he apologized for it.

"The years go by and in some ways you stay the same, but

your experiences are so different..." Michael thought about Kenny Smith and how jealous he had been of the guy and how amazed he had been that Sarah had married him. He wanted to ask her why she had done it; she had surely known the stories about what his family were up to. Had she thought that because Kenny was different he was better?

"And sometimes it's because of choices you've made; at other times it seems to be because of what other people have chosen to do." She remembered this idea from a class she had had at college, but she couldn't quite remember how the teacher had put it; better than this, anyway...

Michael suddenly felt he should say something that showed his concern for her. Life had not been easy for her since she had left school.

"So... how is Kenny?" Where the question had come from, he didn't know, but as the words came out, he was quite pleased with himself.

It wasn't quite like a red rag to a bull to mention her ex husband's name; it was more like throwing water onto an oil fire: taken entirely off-guard and with memories stirred up of being taunted with the "Sexy Sarah" tag, in her heat there was an immediate explosion of emotion, bringing regret, anger, sadness and huge embarrassment. She had been trying very hard to maintain a veneer of professional detachment but Michael's simple four-word question ripped it off and laid the reality of her past hurt bare and obvious before them both. Tears immediately filled her eyes and she sobbed loudly. She bowed her head and tried to quiet herself.

Michael realized his mistake with horror. He sprang up as if to right an upturned milk jug, but then stopped himself. This was Sarah, not Emma! But something propelled him forward anyway and he perched on the arm of her chair and stretched his arm round her shoulders. How he longed to hold her and show her what he felt for her.

"Sorry... sorry..." he mumbled. Her shoulders stiffened against him and he withdrew. He stood up and felt like a complete idiot as she sobbed, now quietly, into her knees. Slowly he reversed back into his seat and as he did so she got up. It looked like a seesaw, he thought. She said something like "just be right back" and went out of the room. Michael sat in his seat and thought about leaving, to save her further embarrassment. But leaving would make her feel even worse, he decided. She reappeared a minute or two later. Her eyes were reddened with the tears, but she was putting a brave face on it.

"I'm sorry about that, Michael. I hadn't realized I still had those feelings inside. I've kinda just swept those things under the carpet. Let's make a start, shall we?"

Michael started talking about Emma and him and as he saw Sarah's interested gaze, he spoke even more quickly, explaining every point and detail. She seemed particularly interested in the part where he told her about Emma's night of infidelity with her old flame.

"Why exactly did you feel you should accept that? Is it OK for people to be unfaithful, as long as it's just for one night?"

Michael felt the edge in her question; it was a little like she was challenging him to justify himself. "Well, I did think about ending our relationship then, but she seemed to be genuinely sorry that she had done it..."

"But don't you think the question is: 'Why did she do it?' rather than, 'Is she sorry?'" Sarah seemed to be quite vehement now.

"At the time that's not the way it seemed. She did it 'cos she was a bit drunk." He paused, and decided that honesty would be good at this point; it would show his vulnerable side. "Truth to tell, I was always a bit in awe of Emma. She was kind of... in charge. In a sense, I had deserved it."

"Deserved what?" Sarah sounded almost angry now. He could feel panic rising up within him, a little as it did with Emma.

"Well, deserved her being unfaithful. I hadn't been very...
attentive, and I guess I felt she needed something else."

Sarah could scarcely believe her ears. She was indeed angry,
but she was alert enough to realize that her questions were
revealing the fact, as was her tone of voice. *What a jerk this guy is!*
she thought. *Does he have no sense of identity, or worth, outside of his
relationship with Emma?* Counseling, which she had got involved
in as a way of helping people and concerning herself with issues
outside of herself, was starting to show her the amazing variety
of human beings and how differently they think, feel and
behave. But she was finding it difficult to conceal the growing
contempt she felt for this wimp of a man. As the silence between
them started to extend uncomfortably she forced herself to think
again about the counseling lessons she had gone to: *Always try to
reflect what the person is thinking, rather than give them advice. They
have their answers inside...*

"Can you think why you might feel you deserved to be
treated like that?" It was almost like she was repeating herself,
but she could think of nothing else to ask.

"To be honest, I've never found it easy to be sure of what to
do or how to react; not like Emma, who always came over as
determined and confident. I admire people like that. Before I
make a decision I have to ask millions of questions first and even
then I don't know for sure what to de, or what to believe."

"D'you think that's maybe why Emma chose you?" the words
were out before she could stop them. That was totally the wrong
question: invasive, assuming, leading and wrong! She was
supposed to help him discover his truth, not suggest answers to
questions he had never thought about.

"That's a very good question, Sarah. A really good question...
Yes, maybe you're right; maybe that's why she chose me. It felt
like that." Michael gave himself permission to have a good look
at Sarah for the first time since she had sat down again. She
looked lovelier than ever now that she had helped him see this

truth. Her rather cold beauty had been animated by her tears and he could see that she was genuinely interested in him. She seemed to be annoyed at the way Emma had treated him: that was good; she was on his side, then.

"Maybe that's something you can reflect on before next time. We should maybe call it a day there. Can you manage the same time next week?"

Michael was taken aback. That was quick! And rather brief... Maybe she wanted to cut things short because of the drama at the beginning regarding Kenny. But he felt confident enough to ask her, somewhat hurriedly, "Yes, that would be great, but er... could we perhaps meet before that... somewhere for a drink maybe, just for a chat?"

Sarah was annoyed. She was trying to be professional here and keep things calm and helpful and this guy seems to just want to chat me up. He had looked a bit strange at the start. Was that why? Maybe he fancied her? "I'm sorry, Michael, that wouldn't be appropriate. In the counseling situation, it's important to maintain professional distance."

Appropriate? What kind of a word was that? Her rebuttal had undermined him and further reduced his self-assurance. But he guessed she was right. Maybe after they were finished with the counseling...

"Sure, yes, of course you're right. Sorry. I'll see you next week same time. Thanks."

One thought went through Michael's mind again and again in the days that followed: that Emma had chosen him because he was weak and indecisive. It made sense: she liked to get her own way and he let her do so. But when he stood up to her and refused to move away with her, then she ditched him. This thought allowed him to let go of Emma more easily; she had left town without a further word to him, as if their years together had meant very little to her.

The remaining four counseling sessions passed without

incident; to Michael, Sarah looked as cool and distant as she had always done. It was as if she was playing the role of counselor rather than actually being one.

A few months later a strange coincidence occurred. Michael had been playing darts at his home pub and was standing at the door on his way out. As he held the door open for a young couple to enter, he noticed over their shoulder that a tall middle-aged man whom he half-recognized was looking rather flustered as he tried to get into his smart and shiny car. The look of panic on his face was odd, but he did not immediately link this with the fact that Sarah's flat was just across the road.

It's hard to describe the mixture of feelings Michael had after he looked away from Sarah and back to Graham's silver car, negotiating its way out of the parking spot near the pub. He was horribly jealous; he had dealt with his feelings for Sarah by convincing himself that she was a cold fish who had been so hurt by her unfortunate liaison with Kenny Smith that she was unlikely to be available for anyone else for a long time to come. The sudden thought that she was having an affair with Pastor Graham unraveled that conclusion and stirred up his longing for her once again.

It also stirred up a kind of anger with himself: since she had after all been available, why had he failed to take advantage of his opportunity when it arose? Memories of the first counseling session filled his mind, when his throat had dried up and he had been unable to speak. How embarrassing that had been! Perhaps it was that which had changed Sarah's mind; perhaps until then she had been quite 'up for it' but he had come over as something of a speechless weirdo.

He walked down the road towards his house. He started "working mental overtime" as Emma used to call it. How long had this liaison been going on? He had noticed the car a couple of times already. Michael wondered if Sarah had started seeing Graham McCreadie at the time of his counseling sessions with her; if so, she was a cunning one indeed! Had she not rebuffed him by telling him that a counselor dating a client was "inappropriate"? How much more inappropriate was it that she was now dating the pastor? He found himself becoming quite angry at the immorality of it. Michael had a fairly simple view of the world, but it was also a moral one and he disliked people who fell foul of it. His jealousy added a bitter flavor to his sense of unfairness.

He was very disappointed in Pastor Graham. Not that he knew him well, but from what he had heard he was highly-regarded. The Baptists made quite an issue of personal morality (more than his own Anglican church, anyway) so it was all the more regrettable that their pastor should be guilty of something like this.

Maybe of course he was wrong; maybe he had put two and two together and got five. He rounded the corner at the bottom end of the High Street. Perhaps she had some issues of her own that needed to be sorted and Graham McCreadie was helping her. He was, after all, a pastor. He would have a lot of experience in helping people in times of crisis... But no, there was no mistaking Sarah's look up at that window: it was a look of love, he told himself. Besides, is it normal for a minister to do visits to a single woman at 10 pm?

Then he began to get excited that he had uncovered a scandal. Perhaps the papers would be interested: they always liked a juicy tale of naughty vicars and the like; this was even juicier – a Baptist! Maybe he could make some money from it. But the thought died as quickly as it had come to life: he wouldn't dare to approach the papers, even anonymously.

As he rounded the final corner, his thought was a simpler one: *why not me?* He asked himself what Sarah saw in Pastor Graham that she didn't see in him. He was a middle-aged man: was it his maturity? Perhaps it was the very fact of Graham's unavailability: some women are strongly attracted to distant, hard-to-get men. (He had seen that in a film on TV recently in which Richard Gere played a psychiatrist.) Besides, it was probably exciting to carry on an illicit affair. Sarah had had a fairly rough time of it with Kenny Smith so she could do with a thrill in her life. He couldn't blame her; she wasn't the guilty one.

But a Baptist minister?

When he spoke about it, none of the three people listening to his story came to the same conclusion. Geoff told him that his own feelings for Sarah were clouding his judgment. Mrs. Grant, an aunt who attended the Baptist church, told him that Pastor Graham would under no circumstances do something so wrong. His father completely believed him and even urged him to spill the beans. But then he added: *"Mind you, they'll either hate you or ridicule you in every church in town!"* Michael did nothing. A week or two later a little-believed story about Pastor Graham seeing Sarah went around town; it was said in the Baptist Church that this was the devil trying to undermine his wonderful ministry. But neither Graham nor Sarah heard the rumor; and of course Anne would have been the last to hear.

The months went by and Michael started to doubt his own observations – had he really seen his car? Had she really been up at the window in her nightgown? Had she had really blushed when he mentioned Graham's name? Finally he decided that he had indeed been mistaken.

Four years later his father was diagnosed with skin cancer. Michael was thrown into turmoil. By now he was sharing a flat with Geoff Stripes in the center of the town. His mother was calm and serene, but he could sense that his father was scared. They talked brightly about the treatment which the specialist had suggested as if it afforded them grounds for optimism, but behind Tom's calmness Michael could see a deep fear of dying.

One evening Michael's phone rang. It was his father. "Michael, would you mind if I came with you to church on Sunday?"

"Of course not, I'd be delighted if you came with me. I can

pick you up."

"But would you mind if we didn't go to that Fellowship place? Could we go to the normal church?"

Michael had settled into a routine of attending his home church once a month, and the Fellowship of Christ the rest of the time.

"Of course we can, no problem. It's at 11, so I can pick you up at 10:30."

The service was a very routine one, but Tom was evidently deeply moved. He didn't look up at the end of the service, but remained seated, head bowed, apparently praying. Michael sat slightly awkwardly, not knowing what to do, whether to get up and speak with people or sit by his father's side. The minister approached and sat next to Tom. Michael had grown a little distant from him over the past few years, because he thought he was slightly wishy-washy and not fervent enough. But now, as he tenderly placed an arm around Tom's shoulders, there was no mistaking his pastoral warmth.

Michael couldn't hear what was said as Tom turned his bowed head towards the minister, so he slid cautiously along the pew and left his father with the minister.

It was fully half an hour later that Tom appeared at the door of the hall, where two men were stacking chairs along with Michael. In silence, father and son left the church and walked to Michael's car. He set off towards his parents' house, and was within sight of the end of the road when Tom spoke. "Don't take me back. Go out and round past the Rec." Michael drove the car past the recreation ground, where the road left the town and open country began. "Could you pull over there at the lay-by?" his father asked.

When the car had stopped, Michael kept on looking straight ahead, sensing that his father had been crying and wanting to spare him embarrassment.

"While the service was going on I knew that God was with me.

He said that everything was going to be OK."

"What, you mean, that He's going to heal you?" said Michael, trying to suppress his excitement.

"He didn't say that. Just that everything was going to be OK. And your minister said the same thing. I've got this calmness inside – like your mum has." There was a smile on Tom's face that brought tears to his son's eyes.

The cancer spread very quickly and Tom's treatment was changed to palliative care. He died eight months after his first diagnosis. Michael went to see the minister to thank him for taking the funeral. "You know, Dad's death has been a real turning-point for me..." he began.

"In what way?" asked the minister.

"Well, here I am thirty years old and for the first time in my life I know that I can really trust God to do the best thing. Not the thing that I want, but the best thing."

Michael came to more deeply understand what Jesus meant when he said, *Then you will know the truth, and the truth will set you free* (**John 8:32**). Until the crisis of his father's illness he had been searching for something solid, reliable and authoritative which he had thought was truth, but was not. His faith had been real, but had been too much of a conscious, mental thing. He had trusted in God in a wishful way, more in hope than expectation. But now his trust was fuller, and he had been set free from the constant striving for security and assurance which had been the hallmark of his life until then. And if you had asked Michael to explain how it was he could trust God now; how he knew that God was there with him, he would have said: *"I just know it; that's all!"*

Spiritual Exercises for 6s

1   As you pray, to quiet your mind from the busy thoughts, try using written prayers. As you read them aloud, really focus on their meaning and pray them with genuine belief.

2   It's been suggested (Riso and Hudson, *Wisdom of the Enneagram*, p. 250) that most 6s have an "inner committee" – people who give them advice about all manner of issues. Are you aware of yours? Who is on it? Why?

3   Feelings of inferiority are common for many 6s. Meditate and reflect on this truth: "God has given you all you need and has already enabled you to do all you need to do." If you hear contrary voices as you reflect on this, consciously respond: "No, that is not true."

4   *Can any one of you by worrying add a single hour to your life?* **Matthew 6:27.** Emma called Michael's frantic thinking "working mental overtime". Can you see this at work in yourself? What does it feel like? Does it help or hinder you?

5   *... nor will people say, 'Here it is,' or 'There it is,' because the kingdom of God is in you* (**Luke 17:21**). Reflect on these words of Jesus'. Try to imagine what it would be like to trust that God is giving assurance within your heart and mind. Invite God to make you sure. (You may need to do this several or indeed many times.)

6   The writer Ginger Lapid-Bogda suggests a helpful exercise: instead of asking someone else for advice, ask yourself: "*If someone else were coming to me with a similar request for advice, what advice would I give?*" (*Bringing Out the Best...* p. 250)

7   It is not uncommon for 6s to ask for advice but to disguise it as "seeking counsel" from other believers. Do you

notice this in yourself? Try to reflect on why you do this, rather than trust your own judgment.

Catherine's Story: Type 7

Praise the LORD from the earth,
you great sea creatures and all ocean depths,
lightning and hail, snow and clouds,
stormy winds that do his bidding,
you mountains and all hills,
fruit trees and all cedars,
wild animals and all cattle,
small creatures and flying birds,
kings of the earth and all nations,
you princes and all rulers on earth,
young men and women,
old men and children.
Psalm 148:7–12

Sandy slammed the door shut behind him. It was like the ending of one of those cheap soap operas on the TV, Catherine reflected. Sandy had always been a bit of a drama-queen, exaggerating things and reacting emotionally – like the time he had found her in the Red Lion sitting on Brian Davis' knee.

"There were no seats left," she explained.

"Yeah, right. Was there no place to stand either? Have you any idea how humiliating it is for me when you do that?"

"Do what?"

"Flirt with guys," he spat out, angry now, and feeling justified.

"It would be flirting if there was anything to it, but there wasn't, and isn't."

The truth was, she had enjoyed the effect she had had on Brian when she sat on his knee: he was embarrassed, but delighted. Brian had long been a Katie fan, and during one episode of adolescent infatuation even considered going to church to see her and spend time with her. For Catherine, it was the feeling of 'running near the edge' that excited her more than the mild sexual *frisson*. She loved to confound others' expectations of her and do the unexpected. From her perch on Brian's knee she had felt she was doing something cheeky and somewhat risqué. But Sandy had reacted with his usual hysteria and had even spoken to her mother about it!

Pushing the envelope had always been a thrill for Catherine. The head teacher thing – what, ten years previously? – was a case in point: he had been so sexist! He had even suggested that as the pastor's daughter she should set and maintain a higher standard of behavior than others. Her response, "Well, sir, as head teacher I would expect you to set and maintain a higher standard too! Sexual and religious discrimination in one fell swoop!"

She wrote to the local paper complaining, but instead of publishing the letter the editor phoned the head teacher, who objected vehemently to the letter being published, so it was quietly filed away. Katie, never one to let sleeping dogs lie, went to the newspaper office all guns blazing.

"Is he above criticism because he's the head teacher? Or are you scared of what he might do?"

The editor was actually trembling slightly as he faced the feisty 14 year old in front of him. "Miss, we're not allowed to publish the personal kind of comments you made."

"I'm saying it's shocking that he can get away with discrimination like that and it seems that I have no right to complain."

"I'm sure that there are ways of making your views known within the school, Miss McCreadie. Like the School Board."

The letter was never published and nothing more was done, but the head teacher gave Katie a wide berth from then on. He felt a mixture of loathing and anxiety towards her: he resented the way she seemed to think the rules didn't apply to her, and she was a troublesome child, likely to encourage others to indiscipline too.

Young Katie resented rules, not because she thought she should be exempt or because she felt so special (she didn't) but because they were a restraint to her freedom. When she sensed this, she had a visceral feeling which maddened her and often prompted her to criticize others or justify herself. She could still remember how as a young child she had hated the way her mother often cuddled her for too long, using her adult strength to prolong the physical contact even though Katie was struggling to be free of it.

The slammed door didn't annoy or upset Catherine one bit, and for a moment or two she realized how strange that fact was. Sandy's departure to be with Nadine, his long-time admirer, suddenly freed her from the shackles of a marriage she had agreed to impetuously four years before, and during the three years of its duration she had frequently wondered how she could escape. Sandy's cloying sentimentality sometimes sickened her; his desire to become a father was ridiculous: the very idea of having children hanging on to her legs and preventing her going out! The passionate love she had felt for Sandy at the outset of their relationship had quickly dwindled, and although his very comfortable income had provided them with a large house, two smart cars and handsome holidays each year, the price she was paying in frustration was no longer worth it. As the door closed, she muttered, somewhat blasphemously, "Thank you, Lord."

Sometimes Catherine's thinking was so rapid and scattered that she found herself dealing with two or three sets of anxieties at once. Now, she realized that her mother would be upset that she had split up with Sandy – indeed she had doted on him as the son she had longed for but never had. Worse still, she would need to look upset herself as she told her mother the news, so she would need to work out how to play that. At the same time she would have to face the church, many of whose members had long grave doubts about the advisability of Catherine marrying an unbeliever. At least she would prove them right...

The third set of thoughts which suddenly coursed through her brain were to do with Sandy's possible return. He had never left like this before, but he was after all quite emotional at times and manipulative as well: she wouldn't put it past him to use walking out on her as a ploy. By now he knew she wanted to be rid of him, but she didn't know how serious things were between him and Nadine. What if he came back? She would be back to square one again; he would get the plaudits for doing the decent thing and trying to make things work and she would be cast as the baddie in the scene, whose wild and difficult behavior had upset her kind and successful husband.

In an act that she was to remember with not a little shame, she hurriedly put on her coat, collected her car keys and rushed out to B&Q to buy new locks for the front and back doors. Her neighbor, Brian Cannon from the Fellowship, peered through the curtains of his spare bedroom later that evening and saw her working on the locks by the light of a torch.

"I have the right to do anything," you say—but not every-thing is beneficial. "I have the right to do anything" – but not everything is constructive.
1 Corinthians 10:23

It was the next day that she noticed Tim on the cross trainer at the gym. Tim was another of the men she enjoyed flirting with, but she had a deeper and healthier feeling for him also: she admired his depth and his calmness. Ever since she had read about her Enneagram type 7, she had understood why she felt an almost magnetic draw towards him: on her good days she was like him in his ability to reflect quietly about things in a focused way. He was also quite good-looking. Moreover, for ten years or more she had known he had feelings for her. For the same reason that she had previously stepped back from closeness to Tim – he was slightly boring, after all – she now drawn to him. He was like an anchor of safety and quietness in the midst of the storm of her life.

In the café afterwards he looked so awkward though. She told him straight out about Sandy leaving in order the clear the way for what she wanted to suggest next. She was being pushy – she even felt that energy in herself – but Tim was surely one person no one could object to her becoming friendly with: he was an old school friend, a deacon in the church and a reliable kind of guy. She ignored what she knew of her mother's thoughts about Tim (he was "geekie and a bit weirdo") and her father's (he was something of a sidelines critic with his head in the clouds). Recently her father had started referring to Tim as "Jerry" for a reason that he insisted on keeping to himself.

When she blithely but warmly said, "I really like you, Tim," she was taken by surprise when he picked up his bag to leave. He appeared so discomfited! That wasn't what was supposed to happen. He was meant to say something similar and they would then agree to meet for a meal or something. She panicked, sensing that she was losing the moment: "Can I drop by some time?" With great relief she saw him nodding as he walked away.

The next day she got on her bicycle and rode for over an hour down the canal towpath which she had so often ridden along as a child. As she took in the sights and the smells she was intoxicated with the abundance of color, sound and scent. It was this which had so frequently made her mindful of God's power and glory: the excess of everything – not a few flowers, but thousands of them grew, wild, along the side of the path, and the plants in the hedgerows grew with such fecundity that they competed with each other for light, heat and water. Once, aged nine, she had collected blackberries from the bushes that ran alongside the disused railway line now converted into a cycle path: her hands scarcely paused and in an hour she had collected three carrier-bags full.

As she cycled along, she felt the power in her legs forcing the pedals round fast and strong; the late summer warmth enveloped her and she was filled with a sense of well-being and happiness. She felt so fully alive, free from the cloying and smothering clutches of her husband. What luck that he had been the one to go off; maybe Nadine was pregnant; there was a snail crawling down a wet section of broken wall; she could only take one day off work; he would be so angry if he came back and found the locks changed; maybe Tim would want to sleep with her; she wasn't sure about that; the church mustn't get the impression she's happy Sandy left; she would keep her car even though he'd paid for it; the mortgage payments were quite high; there are more brambles... But instead of bringing confusion, these thoughts excited her and added to her sense of the wonderful richness of life. Far, far from her still center of closeness to God, she was thrilled to feel so vibrant and happy.

Her mobile phone rang. Slowing down, she edged it out of her jeans pocket and answered it. It was Brian Davis. "You free for lunch today?" he asked.

As he went to the bar to get the drinks, Catherine reflected that the trouble with Brian was that he was too much like she was herself: energetic, bouncy, talkative, optimistic and often super-ficial. He was also a famous womanizer and, she thought with sudden vehemence, he clearly hadn't grasped the idea that most decent women don't like the idea of being one in a series of conquests. But she liked being with him because he was on her wavelength.

"So how long you off work for?"

"I went to work the day after he left, but the boss thought I should be at home – said I was obviously not focused. Went in the next day and he said the same thing again. I thought I was doing fine. I know I was doing fine. But I thought, blow it, if he think I should be off work I'll do it, so I phoned in yesterday and said I thought he was right and I would take yesterday and today off, go back Monday." Sometimes she heard herself and realized she said too much.

Their conversation darted around topics, as it always did and his eyes darted around her body as they always did. She enjoyed it more than she liked to admit to herself.

As they were getting ready to leave, having paid the bill, he quietly asked: "So, how would it be if I dropped by some time, some evening?"

He had never been so obvious. The thought occurred to her that Brian was good fun to play with, but as a lover he would be awful – selfish, driven and abrupt. "I have a neighbor from the Stasi. I think he monitors my phone calls, I suspect he checks out my rubbish and he certainly would know exactly who you are by the time you ring the doorbell."

"I'll climb over your back fence."

"He has a motion-sensitive spotlight that he brought back from the prison camps he used to run in East Germany. His Doberman will get you. No, Brian, not just now." She asked herself, why could she not say "Not ever either?"

She didn't go to church on the following Sunday: all the sympathetic faces and false expressions of interest, she reflected, would be too much. Besides, her absence would make it look like she was really too upset to come. Instead she went to Mass at a Dominican retreat center some miles away, where she had been a couple of times before.

After the service, Brother Simon approached her as she sat alone at a bare wooden table with a cup of tea. "Good to see you, Kathleen," he said.

"Hey, Simon, pretty good memory, but it's Catherine. How are things in the Dommies?"

She explained her situation to Simon, while he listened silently. She loved this man's centeredness and calm. He claimed he owed much of his inner peace to the Enneagram, which he had taught to both Catherine's father and a deacon, Keith. She concluded: "I love my life, you know? I'm not sad that Sandy's gone: it was a mistake ever marrying him. But why can I never find real peace? Even when I'm tired out I'm still restless."

"The Bible answer is simple. Friendship with the world is the problem. Each one of us has a worldly way of dealing with our pain. Trouble is, it looks like the real deal and usually it's fun."

"I don't see that," she responded. "In what way am I being a friend of the world?"

"You said you thought you were a 7, if I remember right?" She nodded. "Then you're scared of being trapped. Deep inside you think that you can be free by seeing more of the world – more travel, more beauty, more fun, more experience... That's your way of dealing with your pain. But it just enslaves you to yourself – like having your arm shackled to your leg."

"And the answer is?" she asked cheekily.

"I doubt if you're ready for the answer, and I'm not going to give you easy, pat replies to complicated questions. Life's more difficult than that and God alone has the answers you need. You know the Bible anyway, don't you? Don't you know the verse for you? *Then you shall know the truth and the truth will set you free.* **John 8:32**. D'you want it in Greek? Or Latin? That's your answer."

She was angry now and she said nothing. She had come for a quick fix, and Simon had found her out. She became even angrier when she realized how vulnerable she felt. Finally she got up and, looking down at Simon, said meanly and spitefully, "Easy for you to say, hidden way out here in your ivory tower. Thanks for your time." She walked hurriedly away towards her bright red sports convertible.

Don't you know that friendship with the world means enmity against God? Therefore, anyone who chooses to be a friend of the world becomes an enemy of God.
James 4:3–5

At work on Monday – a branch of an American business called Cucina which sold expensive kitchens – she was greeted with a warm handshake from her boss. "You should get a pleasant surprise in your mail, Cathy." She loathed the way he called her "Cathy" but she had never had the guts to tell him. "It's good to have you back." He was a good man, and a kind one. So why, she wondered, did she find him so irritating? Was it his way of always wanting to be helpful? Why did he need to be needed?

At her desk there was a pile of mail waiting for her. The fifth letter confirmed an order for 35 luxury kitchens, for which she would receive commission of a little under £8000. She felt surprisingly little joy at the news. As she poured herself a cup of coffee she mumbled to herself: "Maybe I don't even want to be the world's friend… " She was still annoyed at Simon.

After work she went home, had a quick meal and then drove round to Tim's house. His father answered the door and took her through to the kitchen. He was an amiable and understanding man of around 50, whom she liked and respected a lot. His wife was a different story; she reminded her of her boss. After a few minutes, she asked: "D'you think it's possible to be friends with the world just in your attitude? You know what James says about –"

"Yes, yes, *'the epistle of straw'* Martin Luther called it." He thought for a few seconds. "I would've thought attitude has to be what James means. After all, he also says we need to love our neighbors and give generously, so it can't be that he's saying that kind of friendship with the world is wrong."

"But I don't think I'm very materialistic… lots of my non-Christian friends think that I'm totally last century and as for going to church…"

"Has this got anything to do with Sandy leaving?" Tim's father asked.

"Maybe it has. I don't know."

"Well, I'm no great Bible expert – you need to ask your dad if that's what you want – but I think what James meant was that we shouldn't try to find our joy and peace in the world, 'cos we won't find it there. Plus, that kind of attitude of mind will take us away from God, like being his enemies. I think that's what he meant."

Sometimes Catherine experienced things and felt the importance of them later. Her capacity to ask questions and to always want more meant that she often was in a kind of internal overload. But she remembered his words.

When she finally saw Tim an hour or so after arriving at the house, she was relaxed and, for once, a little reflective. She had come to ask Tim out on a date, but somehow she lacked the confidence to just ask him outright. But she had a real love for Tim, quite apart from the frivolous flirting she often engaged in with him. She wasn't sure why she loved him, but she knew that it wasn't like the love she had had for Sandy.

"I meant what I said at the gym, about really liking you," she said, frankly.

"We've been pals for ages," Tim responded. "You're like my big sister."

Catherine's heart sank; that wasn't what she wanted to hear. In a wicked moment the thought came to her to say out loud that now that Sandy had left, it needn't stay that way.

She replied, "Yes, I guess I am. What you doing Sunday after church?"

She enjoyed Tim's company the following Sunday afternoon even more than she had imagined she would. He had a stillness about him which made room for her, but which somehow encouraged her to be calm too. As she pulled up in a lay-by overlooking a valley, she wanted to tell him how she felt towards him, and her wish to develop their relationship. But as she tried to find the words, her head fell backwards and she felt her hair swaying slightly in the breeze. Her eyes closed. Tim had made her feel so good about life, she reflected. She wanted to break the invisible barrier that stood between friendship and a deeper intimacy, but she couldn't find the way: she sensed that, if anything, his inner calm had taken him even further away from her. He was "blissed out" as Simon once called it.

Fifteen minutes passed as they sat there drinking in the springtime green of the countryside laid out before them. Catherine looked at Tim and their eyes met. She half nodded as if to signal that she had sensed the specialness of the moment, and started up the car. In fact her nod was a resigned acceptance that they would go no further towards sexual love.

Catherine stopped the car in front of her house and they stepped out. She approached Tim and he opened his arms. For a brief moment she wondered if he was, after all, about to kiss her, but he hugged her instead, warmly and tenderly. She loved him indeed with a sisterly love, but still she felt his platonic intimacy as a kind of rebuke to her desire. Sometimes he was too pure!

As he walked away she grew envious of his steadiness and strength. She realized that she desired these qualities for herself even more than she desired him. A thought crossed her mind: did she sometimes want people because of the qualities they could bring her? Sandy's tenderness and love, Tim's inner depth and calm, her father's poise…

That evening she was especially distracted and scattered. She scanned through the dozens of TV channels, but found nothing to retain her attention. She ate a snack, then got ready her gym gear and went out. After a quarter of an hour she was bored, showered and drove to her parents' house. They were out – it was the time of the evening service. She left again and drove to the Red Bull, where she had met Brian Davis. She scanned the room, but there was no one she recognized. She sat by herself at the fireside end of the bar, idly reading the glossy supplement from the paper.

"Escaping the Stasi-man?" It was BD himself, but his voice made her shiver inwardly; he was so greasy and suggestive, like a dirty old man. He was facing her now, leaning slightly against her leg and trapping her against the wooden bar.

"Hey, Brian," she responded, glad that she had at least found someone to talk to. He was looking straight into her eyes and his face was closer than she felt comfortable with – something she had often done herself, with Tim for instance.

"So, is little miss lonely surviving the single life? Or has he come back? Is that why you're here?" he laughed cynically. He now had his left hand on her right knee.

"No, Sandy's not back, and yes, I'm enjoying being single again. Meeting up with good friends, doing what I want…"

A rather overweight girl with dyed blond hair and maybe ten years younger than Brian appeared out of nowhere and immediately tugged at Brian's right hand, pulling him away. His expression changed instantly, leering at the girl, who sneered at Catherine aggressively as the two of them sashayed away to the other end of the bar. Catherine felt sullied and cheapened: why did he hang out with girls like that? She finished her drink and drove home.

That evening she felt broken up and unsettled, unable to focus. She slept badly and woke unrefreshed. She arrived at work tetchy and unsociable, but an e-mail from the American head office suddenly focused her attention and excited her once again.

"So what's the deal? And why should I accept?" she asked her boss.

"Cucina are setting up a big new network in Chicago and they want proven sales people to set it up. Seemingly the guy in charge has a thing for English saleswomen – says they really click with American men… "

"And what'll I get paid?"

"Bucketloads: starting on 60K, plus commission: you'll be earning double what you get here."

"Why d'you want rid of me?"

"Truth? I get nice personal bonus in my salary for finding you, plus in my budget I get what you earned this last year."

All day she schemed and planned, anticipating the possibilities and thinking through the changes in her life. Chicago! Sandy would be livid. Her dad would be proud; her mum would be anxious. As she thought about it, she realized that there was no one who would hold her back.

"Don't you think this is a bit too quick, darling?" asked her mother that evening.

"Sandy's been leaving for well over a year. I've been prepared. Plus this is an opportunity I'm not likely to get again in a hurry. The contract's only for 12 months anyway..."

Graham knew better than to try to talk his daughter out of anything she had made up her mind on. When his wife left the room to answer the phone, he explained to Catherine: "She doesn't understand how it can be so easy for you to up and leave. She feels it's like you don't love her enough. But that's the way it is with 7s..."

She felt a strong surge of love for her father: he not only understood, he could also deal with the fallout her actions caused with other people. Plus he didn't seem to be upset by her energy and drive.

A little over six weeks later Catherine flew to Chicago, with two large suitcases and a lot of excitement. The company had found her a tiny flat in a shiny sleek new block in the South Shore area of the city not far from the lake, for which she would pay a huge rent and ridiculously high monthly charges for the doorman and the other fancy facilities in the building.

Her father was right: she found adapting to Chicago lifestyle remarkably easy and she enjoyed the attention from her colleagues, who treated her as a sales specialist and seemed to show extra respect to her due to her Englishness and her accent. Her boss, whose name appeared to really be Tiny Hughes, liked her instantly and adopted her into his own large family, inviting her to their Thanksgiving meal and for Christmas and New Year.

The months passed very quickly as Catherine was kept frenetically busy, often starting work with a breakfast meeting at 7:30 and not ending until drinks in the local bar at 9 in the evening. She had been given an allowance to return home once during the year, but she used it to visit southern California in late January, travelling with an older single woman who worked in the same section.

She quickly discovered Willow Creek church, west of the city, following advice from her father. She loved the buzz of the place, the huge car parks and the feeling of success and efficiency that was everywhere. She joined up to a home group in her neighborhood – one of the other members worked for Cucina – and was welcomed like a special guest.

She dated Jack, one of the home group members, for two months; then she saw Sanjay, a young computing student five times until his awkwardness with her became annoying. There were three other men whom she saw occasionally, one of whom took her to his parents' New Hampshire home for a weekend. She was horrified to be introduced as "my lovely partner" as if they were engaged. She refused to see him again. A succession of five one night stands followed.

The year was nearly finished when she was called into Tiny Hughes' office. "Can I talk you into another six months with us?" he asked.

"No need to talk me into it – oh, no."

"What?" Tiny asked, surprised.

"I realized too late there that what I should've done was say no, and wait for you to make me an increased pay offer to persuade me to stay. Sorry, Titch."

"You missed a trick there, Catherine. But I really don't want you to leave. I like your style. And you fit in here like a hand in a glove. Just until Thanksgiving…"

The six months became nine and then a further six followed to cover for Tiny's absence setting up a new office in Delaware. She had spent something over two years in Chicago.

She caught the night flight back to Heathrow. Her father collected her from the station, carrying a large "Welcome Home" balloon and drove her to the manse. The next day she spent with her parents, sharing experiences and showing them photographs. They both seemed more excited in her return than they were interested in what she had done.

Almost at once she dropped into what appeared to be a mild depression. The boring sameness of the town annoyed her, her old job was dull in comparison and she missed the bright energy and optimism of Chicago. She badly wanted to move back into her house, but the tenants would not be leaving for three months. Most of her friends seemed to be either too busy or not interested. Several hadn't known she had been abroad. She started feeling insignificant.

She picked up the phone late one evening. "Tim, it's Catherine. I'm back! Did you know?"

"I didn't, no. Was it good?"

"Awesome," she said. "Hey, are you busy?" she asked.

"Just reading. Why?"

"Come for a drive. I need to talk."

He was standing outside his parents' house shivering in thin jacket.

"Got the old car back again, then?"

"Yes," she replied. "Dad took it for a spin now and again and kept it from seizing up."

They talked idly for a few minutes as she drove around aimlessly. Finally she stopped in the lay-by outside the secondary school.

"Come with me to Greece," she said, hoping to surprise him into agreeing.

"I'd love to, but you know I'm engaged now and I somehow

think that Jill wouldn't be too happy about me going on holiday with someone else."

"I'll tell her we won't have sex – that'll make it OK. She likes me."

Tim said nothing for a minute. He knew that Jill loathed Catherine and saw her as a rival for Tim's affections. "I'm sorry, I really can't. Besides, I've all my holiday used up now."

Tim seemed to Catherine to have closed the door on their friendship and in the days that followed she was even more subdued and depressed-looking. She found a cheap last-minute flight to Corfu and left the next day. She was booked into a small hotel a few miles north of the main town, Kerkyra.

Early in the morning two days later she caught a bus towards the foot of the Pantokratoras. She started making her way up the rough track winding up the mountain. She could see little of the rest of the island until she reached the disused monastery near the summit. She skirted round it, and made her way to the top. A chill easterly wind from Albania hit her with force as she looked over towards Barbati. The hillside below her was grey and barren, in stark contrast to the green of the rest of the island.

Celtic tradition has it that there are 'thin places' where the presence of God breaks through more powerfully than elsewhere. As she stood on that hill's edge she reflected that this was one such place. All her sadness and frustration fell away, as if blown away in the chill February wind and she sensed within her a profound gratitude to God for the gift of her life. Tears flowed unrestrained down her cheeks while she breathed great lungfuls of air deeply in, as if to nourish the peace she had suddenly discovered.

"I need nothing more than this," she muttered, wiping her wet face with her scarf. In the stillness of this 'thin place' she sensed an inner calm which she had never known before. The easterly wind, like a spirit, blew refreshment deep into her and a brilliant alive-ness pervaded her being. She experienced a depth

within her heart and soul and mind where she felt an extraor-
dinary contact with the moment and its Creator. "I need nothing
more than this," she repeated.

Spiritual Exercises for 7s

1   "Sometimes Catherine's thinking was so rapid and scattered that she found herself dealing with two or three sets of anxieties at once." This kind of mental activity may excite you, but can you see how it harms you?

2   "Young Katie resented rules... because they were a restraint to her freedom." Make a list of three rules you dislike and then find three positives about each one.

3   Some 7s find it very easy to let go of a relationship because they are not really in touch with their feelings about the other person. Find somewhere you can be on your own, out of contact. Focus on someone you like or love and try to sense what you really feel for him/her. Note this down.

4   Like Catherine, many 7s have few friends with whom they can be wholly honest, vulnerable and open. Is there someone whom you could confide in like this? Do you dare to be accountable to him/her? If not, why not?

5   The prophet Isaiah speaks loud and clear to the 7's restless yearning for experiences which bring no satisfaction: *Why spend money on what is not bread and your labor on what does not satisfy? Listen, listen to me and eat what is good and you will delight in the richest of fare* (**Isaiah 55:2**). What makes it so hard for you to listen to God's voice rather than your own?

6   "If we cannot be with our pain, we cannot be with our joy." (*Wisdom of the Enneagram*, p. 285.) What pain are you avoiding? Name it in prayer and hand it over to God. You may need to do this several, or many times.

7   Blake wrote about seeing "eternity in a grain of sand." As a spiritual exercise, sit quietly and consider something in your environment – a flower or a pattern or an object. Spend two minutes focused on it. If your attention

wanders, just notice that fact and bring your attention back.

8   Gratitude is a key virtue of the 7. Make a list of the important things in your life for which you are thankful and, with each one, tell God in prayer: "I have enough. Thank you."

Grace's Story: Type 2

⁴⁰And if anyone wants to sue you and take your shirt, hand over your coat as well. ⁴¹If anyone forces you to go one mile, go with them two miles. ⁴²Give to the one who asks you, and do not turn away from the one who wants to borrow from you.
Matthew 5:40–42

This is love, not that we have loved God, but that He loved us...
1 John 4:10
... you have been set free from sin
Romans 6:22

Grace was one of those people about whom no one had a bad word to say. She was attractive, considerate and kind – someone whom many people would turn to in a time of crisis. She was a wonderful listener and a shoulder to cry on. Many of her women friends down the years considered her to be a kind of ideal woman – very approachable, caring for needy people and attractive. Her men friends loved the way she flirted with them and easily touched them on the arm or hand as if hinting at a secret intimacy. She was a people-person.

When Grace started going to the study meeting at the Baptist church, she had been married to Keith for a matter of weeks. She had become friendly with Anne the pastor's wife, but now she was finding her a real nuisance as she stated: "We're all sinners in the eyes of God."

"But I am not a sinner!" Grace repeated. She was getting angry. Her mood wasn't helped by one of the men who contradicted her immediately in a kind of *'I know better than you'* tone of voice: *"Oh yes you are!"* In her mind, sinners were people who robbed and murdered old ladies, or who embezzled large sums of money and that kind of thing.

Grace grew up in what she considered to be a difficult home, where whatever she did was never enough to please her demanding father. He was a critical, exacting and idealistic man who rarely seemed to be happy. When she was eight years old, she brought home from school a painting she had done. It was the first painting she had ever 'worked on': until then her drawings and paintings were the result of a few minutes work, but this painting was of her house and garden, and she had returned to it twice to perfect it. She was very proud of it.

"Grace, it's gorgeous!" said her mother. But she always said nice things about her work, even when they were pretty mediocre. It was her father's judgment that she was keen to receive. A thumbs-up from him would be a real accolade. He had glanced at it briefly on his way past, but he was studying it closely now.

"Yes..." he began in that thoughtful way of his, "the house is the right color and the windows are in the right places..." Grace could feel that there was a 'but' just waiting to strike. "But we haven't got a tree there in the garden." At the same time as she inwardly flinched with the criticism, she sensed her mother tensing up towards her father, ready to defend her. Even at this young age she well knew the sequence of events that would unfold: Grace is proud of something she did, Dad says something critical, Mum defends Grace a bit too much, Dad gets annoyed with Mum. Being the cause and the center of a conflict was worse than receiving her father's criticism.

"She's eight years old, for goodness' sake! It's a beautiful painting!" Her mother touched her gently on the shoulder, to comfort her.

"I know it is. It's great... I didn't..." Her father's annoyance blocked up his words, and he clammed up, angrily. He walked away, leaving Grace sheltered, as it were, under her mother's wing. She hated that, but she couldn't extract herself from her mother's side without upsetting her even more.

Incidents like that played themselves out countless times during her childhood. Some children would have reacted differently, shrugging off her father's criticism with the reflection that he was just an awkward character who didn't mean to be spiteful. Grace strived for her father's approval but time and again she failed to get it. Her successes in swimming (she was county champion for her age group three years running) won her as many negatives as positives: *"Well done, Annie. I'm sure we haven't seen the best of you yet."* The cruel irony was that she didn't like swimming – she was doing it for him because not so far inside her heart she longed for his approval.

Aged 16 she had made ever more fanciful excuses to her boyfriend so that she didn't have to bring him home, anxious that her father would find fault with him too. He never found out that she had dated Rob for 18 months and she had loved him very much.

Grace grew up believing what her mother believed: she would be rewarded with love when she did something kind. She learned that you can earn love, or deserve it; when you do kind things to others, you tend to get good things back. Her favorite primary teacher used to say: "You scratch my back and I'll scratch yours," and Grace agreed that this was a lovely way to see it.

As a child of seven or eight she would play in her bedroom with half an ear for the washing machine cycle ending in the kitchen below, so that she could run downstairs and take out the washing for her mother. She would eat her first course quickly and pass on dessert, especially if they had guests, so that she could collect the plates and sometimes even wash them before the end of the meal. She had a diary which she kept in her bottom drawer with a note of every birthday she could find out, including two of her teachers. If she couldn't afford a card, she would send a note or sometimes just say "happy birthday" in passing.

From an early age she got the reputation of being a very caring and loving person who was 'wise beyond her years' and far more mature than her peers.

So now, aged 24 and sitting in the informal church meeting, Grace didn't want to think of God as judgmental and critical in the way her father was. She wanted to think of God as a very kind uncle who understood why people did bad things, rather than told them off all the time. She wanted God to be nice, that's all. When she heard the words *"all have sinned..."* she heard her father's voice and not a loving God. Besides, she was herself a kind, generous and, in the eyes of many, a truly Christian woman, not a sinner. Neighbors needing a lift to hospital went to Grace, who took them without question; she was a shoulder to cry on for many of her friends; at times it seemed she was almost looking for people to look after. The notion that she was a sinner was ridiculous!

"Why was Paul so down on people?" she said, almost angrily. She hated the way that this disagreement was making her feel, but she couldn't just say nothing. She almost subconsciously felt she was protecting God from the wrong impression these people were giving.

But Anne was persistent: "It's not that Paul was down on people. He was trying to prompt them to change and grow. His real thing is about being transformed by the Holy Spirit."

"Well, it doesn't encourage me very much to want to change. It's not exactly good psychology, I mean is it? Tell people how rotten they are and then say 'Get better!'" She was into her stride. She felt also as if she was standing up for people, like her, who had received enough criticism to last a lifetime.

"OK, Grace. Think of it this way. It's a diagnosis, not a criticism. If you go to your doctor he needs to tell you what's wrong so that you can then do something about it. What kind of a doctor would just say, "Oh, you're fine!" even though he knows you've got a serious but very treatable disease?"

Grace sat back in the sofa, exhausted and a little defeated.

There was a kind of small bell ringing inside her head also about her husband, Keith. Once or twice she had noticed how critical he could be – like her father. She had read somewhere during her nursing degree course that men typically ended up marrying women like their mothers, while women married men like their fathers. It seemed to be happening to her, but maybe that was the way it had to be and she had to just get used to it.

At the hospital where she worked as a nurse Grace recently got her first black mark in an assessment. The ward sister had complained that Grace was spending too much time doing work that was properly the nursing auxiliary's job and not enough on the necessary drudgery of correct record-keeping and administration. When Sister had said this to her, reading from the sheet she had written, Grace stifled her tears by blinking hard. Behind her smiling and understanding face she was fiercely angry. She had come into nursing because she loved caring for people, not to be an administrator. Sister, who had evidently fewer people-skills, would be quite happy sitting in her office and playing on the computer, but not Grace.

She locked herself in the canteen toilets to have a cry. Sometimes when you help others, she sobbed silently to herself, people take it the wrong way – deliberately or not. How can she get told off for giving extra care to patients? She remembered what happened when she was 14. Three new Asian pupils had started in her class. Two were twin sisters, the third was their cousin. She noticed that they seemed totally at a loss in the big comprehensive school. She approached them as they stood together outside the classroom near the door.

"Is this is much bigger school than your old school?" She had wanted to say "the school where you're from" but she had thought this might remind them that they were immigrants.

"Oh no, much smaller. Our old school had 2,487 pupils. This one has under 1,200, I believe."

Grace was annoyed that her friendly opener had been turned into something else: it was like they were showing off now. But she persisted.

"If I can help you getting settled in, just let me know. I can tell you about the teachers."

"Getting around the school is very confusing," the cousin said. "Maybe we follow you to classes?"

"No problem," Grace said, smiling her best smile. But none of the three of them smiled back. This was hard work.

The hard work continued for some weeks, as she helped them with their homework and checked that they had laid out their science project in the correct format. She made three photocopies of some of her biology notes and handed them to them, but they didn't seem very appreciative.

The helping stopped when end-of-year exams came round. The twins came top of the class in four subjects and in the top five in everything else. Grace was languishing around the middle of the class, as usual. She finally realized that the three new girls thought she was not very bright. Even at the tender age of 14, she knew that she didn't enjoy being with people who didn't need her in some way and she hardly ever spoke with them again.

She unlocked the toilet door, washed her eyes in cold water and went back onto the ward, taking care to report back to the office base and write up nursing notes. She smiled warmly at Sister as she passed her.

She was brought up in a northern city and when she went to university to study nursing, she met Keith who was from the Midlands. She admired the way he stood up for what he believed, but he was also vulnerable and he seemed to appreciate the way she cared for him. She also liked the way he looked at her: he found her very sexually attractive, but when he said this he also told her that he didn't believe in sex before marriage. She hadn't expected him to say this and half smiled involuntarily. Suddenly she realized that he might think less of her if he realized that she wasn't a virgin, so she quickly nodded even as she thought about it. "I totally agree. I mean, totally," she averred, and then wondered if she had sounded too keen.

He started taking her to the lively Baptist church he went to on Sundays and she liked many of the people she met there. The whole feel of the place seemed to click with her – people who cared for others and really loved each other. The main stumbling block was that she didn't believe in God, but oddly enough that didn't seem to matter much to her. Religion, she believed, was a way of keeping people on the straight and narrow. It gave people a reason to be nice to each other. She didn't need reasons to be nice; it was in her temperament. She was no more interested in theology than a mathematician is interested in the color of numbers.

She quickly became involved in the team that gave out soup and rolls to homeless people in the city. She would sit and listen to their stories, which broke her heart sometimes. On one occasion the team leader interrupted a conversation she was having to ask her to help dish out the soup. She smiled sadly at the scruffy and smelly man she had been listening to and went back to serving soup. Eventually she spoke with the secretary who organized the schedule and asked if she could be put on as a 'befriender' rather than as a 'food-server'. The others on the team admired the way she put her arm around the old men and kindly touched others on the arm to show her concern and sympathy. Soon many of them had learned her name and looked for her on a Saturday night.

Along with the sense that these homeless people needed her, she had a hidden feeling that many people – even some in the Church – care less about the people than the idea of befriending homeless people. She had a powerful inner drive to show these poor needy people how much she loved them. The fact that they could see this meant that she never missed a Saturday evening unless she absolutely had to.

In Grace's case, the person that everyone saw was rather different from the one she herself knew. They saw a kind, caring and considerate young woman; she sometimes knew herself to be someone who longed to be needed and certainly resented not being thanked. She virtually never showed her anger to others, but she could feel it sometimes like a furnace inside her, glowing for long months, sometimes years after the event that prompted it.

One Sunday she was annoyed by the Bible reading and the sermon.

> *Give to everyone who asks you, and if anyone takes what belongs to you, do not demand it back. Do to others as you would have them do to you.*
> **Luke 6:29–30**

On the face of it, the idea about generosity seemed to be fair enough, but what annoyed Grace was the way that Jesus seemed to be saying it was OK for people to not repay acts of kindness, or even thank the people who did them. And as for doing to others what you wanted them to do to you – well, she hated it when people thought she needed their help, or wanted her to talk about her problems. She was a giver, and receiving was not easy for her. She sensed she couldn't voice her feelings to Keith because he would know some strong principle that would prove she was wrong. But somehow, she felt, you could be right about something and yet not be loving. And surely loving was better than being right?

As the preacher went on, she opened the shiny red Bible under the seat in front of her and looked up her favorite Bible passage. It warmed her heart:

If I speak in the tongues of men or of angels, but do not have love, I am only a resounding gong or a clanging cymbal. If I have the gift of prophecy and can fathom all mysteries and all knowledge, and if I have a faith that can move mountains, but do not have love, I am nothing.
1 Corinthians 13:1–2

In fact, she reflected, doesn't this prove that you can be right and know everything but still not be OK with God if you don't have love? The truth of the matter was that Grace would never admit to wanting thanks for what she did, but others' gratitude was nevertheless her lifeblood; it energized her and gave her a feeling of well-being.

This was precisely why she wanted to care for patients in a hands-on way, rather than write notes and plan treatments for bedsores or write up discharge notes as she was now doing. Sister sat gloating at her from behind the glass front of her office. Grace smiled again in a kindly way, but with her teeth very slightly clenched. The black mark on her report would mean a delay in receiving the next increment in her salary and she was sure that Isobel, the famously nosey nursing secretary, would find out about it and possibly even ask her why she had been penalized in this way.

When she finished her shift she phoned Anne, the pastor's wife and asked if she could meet to talk. "Sure," Anne replied. "How about straight after the study meeting on Thursday?" That was three days away and she would have preferred to meet sooner, but she felt she would appear too desperate or that she was making out the issue was very important if she pressed the point.

"That would be just fine," she replied. She was on an early shift the day after the study meeting, so she could ill afford to stay up late the night before, but she would just need to make do.

Back at the Bible study, Anne was asking her to read. It felt to

Grace like she was rubbing salt into the wound. She began:

> *But now apart from the law the righteousness of God has been made known, to which the Law and the Prophets testify. This righteousness is given through faith in Jesus Christ to all who believe. There is no difference between Jew and Gentile, for all have sinned and fall short of the glory of God...*

Even as she read, she told herself that the passage was in no way about her in any case. It was about Jews and Gentiles and how both were sinners.

The others left the room in little clusters and Grace was left with Anne and Tim, the pastor, who had come in. She explained that she had been penalized by her boss for not writing up notes and for spending too much time with patients. Anne was very understanding and tutted in disapproval, concluding with, "Well, that's just ridiculous! I mean isn't it, Tim? Fancy paying a nurse less for spending time with patients!"

Tim was quiet for a long time. She could tell that he was less persuaded of her case than Anne had been, who in any case was probably making up for annoying her in the Bible study meeting.

"What d'you think, Tim?" his wife asked.

He looked at Grace for what seemed like a minute before he answered.

"Why do you do it?" he asked. "Why do you spend so much time with the patients?"

"Because I don't like writing up notes," she answered, quickly.

"That's not really an answer," Tim countered. "There are lots of other things you could do – like reading books or taking temperatures or handing out drugs. What's so good about talking with patients?"

"Well, it makes me feel good," she replied, slightly surprised to hear herself say it. Tim was nodding as if he had expected the answer.

"Do they need you to talk to them?"

"Well, I'm about the only one who does really communicate with them. Yes, I think they do need me. Maybe that makes me feel good." Tim nodded again, but she didn't like this feeling of being understood; she felt uncomfortable delving into her emotions.

"Do you get tired out?"

"I'm a nurse. Of course I get tired!"

"I didn't mean it that way. I meant, Do you sometimes feel that there's no end to the work you need to do and the people who need your help?"

It was Grace's turn to look long and hard at Tim. His gaze was unwavering. Anne was blinking on the sofa. The phone rang twice and then the answering machine clicked in and she heard Tim's disembodied voice floating down the hall.

She smiled weakly in a way that signaled to Tim that he had put his finger on something Grace would not or could not discuss. She thanked them both for their time, explained that she had an early shift and left.

"So how did the Bible study go? You're a bit late," Keith asked when she got home.

"It was fine, but it kind of dragged on a bit at the end." She wished she could explain to Keith how she had felt at work, but she sensed that he would not take her side. Then she had second thoughts, sat down on a kitchen stool and laid out what had happened. There were tears in her eyes when she finished.

"That's terrible," Keith said at last. "She's awful, that Sister. You're the most caring and kind person I know. If I was in hospital I'd want you to nurse me any day."

She laughed with relief and got up to hug him. She was suddenly hugely grateful for his support and understanding in the way that someone is when they feel outnumbered and yet in the right.

She was baptized a few months after this bible study and

became a member of the church. She had felt in her element, in this church back in Keith's hometown, just as she had done in her own: there were so many opportunities to serve and show love. In truth, she had qualms about the hardline ideas of the pastor and some of the elders: that Jesus is the only way to God, that Jesus died as a sacrifice in place of others and of course that everyone is a sinner. She felt that these ideas helped them in some way to make sense of things and she attached little importance to them: being a Christian for her was about believing God is with you (and after all, God is love) and trying to be kind to others. Mother Theresa was her heroine.

The problem at work did not go away, nor did Sister. Six months after the last appraisal she was called into her office again, during a quiet afternoon visiting time. She was given a cup of coffee – usually a sign that bad news was coming – and told to sit down with her back to the large glass screen overlooking the ward.

"Grace, it's really lovely having you on the ward and I so much appreciate the way you make contact with patients…" Grace was transported into her childhood and looking at her painting with her father, awaiting his 'but' after the initial positive comments. She loathed the way people used saying nice things as a way to introduce horrible ones.

"But you still have the issue that you had at your appraisal, so I wouldn't be doing my job if I didn't point it out to you."

"I'm not writing enough notes?" Grace smiled as she spoke, hoping that a quick admission might minimize the pain.

Sister closed her file, keeping her finger in the page. "We're a team here, Grace, and we need to be there for each other."

Grace couldn't understand in what way she hadn't "been there" for her colleagues. She often listened to their hard-luck stories and helped them with their man-problems. Sister saw the puzzlement on her face and went on:

"Being a team means working together and not raising false

expectations…"

Grace smiled again, intrigued and quite mystified. Sister tutted quietly and then let the words pour out a bit more quickly than she had intended.

"When you spend an hour with a patient, it makes them think that all the nurses should spend an hour with them. And it makes **all** the patients think that you should spend time with them too. But on top of everything else it makes the other nurses look bad and feel bad because they're not as popular as you."

It was as if the words had solidified in the air and Grace could reach out and study them one by one. She couldn't speak; Sister's words just echoed in her ears and hovered around the small office.

"While you're listening to a patient for half an hour, someone else has to spend an extra half an hour writing up a referral or sending off discharge notes."

Grace knew that two of her colleagues were more than happy to do this, rather than spend time on patient care, which they considered to be beneath them. All she could say, however, was "I see." Her face was solid and fixed in an awkward grin as she left quietly.

The following Sunday one of the deacons' wives spoke to her about a pet project which she had thought Grace could take charge of. She was pushing at a largely open door: "The idea's not a counseling service. That needs trained staff and people come with big expectations. We want to call it a "Care Centre" where people can come and get listened to and find some practical help. It'd be great if you could head it up."

Grace was excited and animated. It occurred to her that there had been a good purpose in Sister's complaint through the week: to prepare her for this new work, which was ten times better.

"Obviously the church can't pay as much as a nurse's salary, but you could do it part-time so that you wouldn't notice the drop in pay…"

"I'm sure Keith would be happy for me to give up work – if it's the right thing, of course." She remembered that she should really pray about it first. "Let me pray about it. When d'you need to know?"

"It's being advertised next week, interviews at the end of the month. Hoping to get started in seven weeks."

Within six months the Care Centre was so busy it required its own telephone line. GPs and social workers sent their problem people along, pensioners dropped in for a chat and advice about their difficulties and occasionally some of the youth group came with relationship problems. Grace recruited three helpers, who did a lot of the phone calls and paperwork, but it was Grace whom everyone came to be with. It was open four days a week and three evenings. To her delight, five of her 'clients' had started coming to church and she had started a women's group meeting with some friends and some of these ex-clients.

It was then she discovered she was pregnant. The prospect of motherhood was delightful, but the idea of giving up her work at the Care Centre was awful – like losing an arm. She had been worrying about it for two weeks when Anne phoned her at the Centre.

"I have the solution, Grace. A really great solution. We open a crèche when the Centre's open so that clients – and you – can leave kiddies there. I'm sure we'll be able to find people to volunteer for it."

When their baby girl was born, Keith agreed to Grace's suggestion regarding her name – Elisa. "We'll pronounce the 's' like a 'z'," she explained.

"Don't you think it's nicer with an 's'?"

"Maybe, but with a 'z' it sounds like Hebrew for 'God's helper'. Isn't that nice?" Keith agreed that it was nice.

Over the next few months Keith realized something about his wife: when her caring attention was taken by someone new, she could turn away from her previous focus with frightening suddenness. Previously the Centre had taken the place of her work and a few of her evenings and as a result Keith had started doing the weekly shopping on his way home from the office and when she was out he would wash and iron their clothes. But now that she had a baby, he sometimes felt he was invisible. She did the same kind things – asking how he'd slept, kissing him when she came home, sympathizing with his troubles at work – but in a distracted way that made it seem more like a gesture than genuine concern.

She also looked like a mother, Keith told himself. As he did the ironing he noticed that many of the clothes she wore were stretched at the seams and in Keith's rather exacting mind that was both ugly and a bit lazy. She was also much less interested in sex. Twice during those few months after Elisa's birth they talked about it: he mentioned that Grace had not lost enough weight and Grace explained that breastfeeding made her a bit plumper than other mums.

In truth, the deeper reason Keith was so annoyed about her weight was that he found her much less sexually attractive than when she was slim, so he was frustrated. It was nearly impossible for him to discuss this with Grace; when he had tried, she had started crying and talked about the demands of running the Centre on top of looking after Elisa. The conversation had ended with her punch line: "After all, you encouraged me to agree to run the Centre." When he reflected on it, he saw himself as a support for her, enabling her to do things which she was gifted at and which he knew to be good for her to do. He could hardly argue with that, but his own deeper needs were increasingly at odds with his conscience and that was a conflict for which he held Grace responsible.

Grace of course sensed this tension in her husband, without being able to pinpoint its precise cause, but she could feel that he was uptight more often now and was critical in a way that she found hurtful. So one morning, arriving at the Centre with no clients in sight, she left Elisa in the crèche, sat at her desk and opened the handmade leather-covered journal which Anne had given her when she had been baptized. She wrote:

Keith is so critical all the time. He makes me nervous in case I do something wrong. Yesterday he watched me making dinner and cleaned up after me as I went. And then after dinner he didn't want to talk because he left to put the dishes in the dishwasher and tidy away everything. Nothing I do is ever good enough for him. I thought the dinner was really nice, and it took me ages to do it after a heavy day at the Centre, but his first comment was, "I prefer it with less salt."

When we went to bed I could feel him watching me get undressed. But when I looked round I could see that it wasn't that he fancied me, but that he was noticing the weight I have put on. It's not a lot, but most of my clothes are a bit tighter now than they were when I got them.

I know he's really idealistic and I admire him for sticking to his principles, but sometimes it seems that he only loves me if I'm good enough to be loved. It's like I have to meet his standards all the time. If I don't, he's really cold with me. Sometimes he doesn't say what's wrong, but I know that I've let him down. He seems to be getting worse.

He went on the other night about the women's group. I don't know if he's jealous that I have set this thing up, but he started up again about how five of them aren't "saved" and that I should lay it on the line about what God expects of them. I would really like to introduce him to them, maybe even get him to come along and give a talk, but I'm worried that he'll upset them by being too religious and demanding.

She stopped writing and read her words to herself. The thought occurred to her that it didn't sound like a spiritual journal, so she added:

I pray that God will give me the strength to see this through and that I can serve him better at home and at the Centre.

She locked the little brass buckle on the top and slipped it into the back of the bottom drawer of the desk.

Within the church Grace was treated with great respect and affection: she always seemed to have time for people, she was tireless in her work and soon there were over a dozen people who had started attending the church as a result. Grace reacted rather differently than most people would imagine: she felt herself growing increasingly annoyed that she gave out so much, but received so little. She saw herself as a kind of servant and she loved to serve, but more and more frequently she asked herself in stifled anger why no one looked after her needs. She actually felt like a martyr – she willingly helped others, but the cost was often her own needs being ignored.

And so life bumped on: the person people saw was ever-giving, caring and loving; the person whom Grace knew herself to be was often irritated and resentful that she was underappreciated. She was never thanked enough.

Some years later, when Pastor Graham left, the new pastor's first sermon was on **1 John 4**, focusing on the verse:

This is love, not that we have loved God, but that He loved us...

The church was packed with people eager to hear their new pastor's voice and to rate his preaching: would he be as good as Pastor Graham?

"What John is saying," the preacher explained, "is that whereas we tend to think about love in human ways – we tend to love people who are loveable – real love comes from God alone, and His love is of a radically different kind from ours. He doesn't love us in order to get us to be nice to him, as we often do, but he loves us simply because that's what he's like; that's what he is."

Sometimes we hear things that have a deep inner truth and whose importance we acknowledge without consciously realizing it. This was the case with Grace that day. She stored Pastor John's thought away in her memory and wrote it in her spiritual journal. And yet, although she was deeply touched, she wasn't changed. Deep down inside she was feeling, "I wish I could know that God loved me that much!" but she couldn't reach in and realize it. It was locked away inside her as surely as her brass-buckled diary was.

It was years later, when she held her first grandchild in her arms that the key was finally turned and that profound thought had its impact upon her psyche. As she looked at the little child the thought finally struck her: *This is how God loves us.* All her life she had striven to win others' love – probably because she had been unsure, deep down, that she was loveable or even that God truly loved her. But now as she adored this little baby just as he was, she sensed herself in God's arms and really knew his love.

The next day, she phoned the man whom she had arranged to meet for a counseling session that afternoon and explained that she needed to spend some time reflecting and praying. "I need some 'me-time'," she explained. She had never once done anything like this, putting her own needs first and being honest about it rather than making excuses.

She walked home and simply reflected on the fact that God is love. It was a warm sunny day and she blinked in the afternoon sunlight at such a simple thought, amazed that it had taken her all these years to see it, feel it and truly know it in her heart. Here she was in her fifties: she was a child again – broken, failing and sinful – but unconditionally loved by her Father.

Spiritual Exercises for 2s

1   Grace decided to phone the man "whom she had arranged to meet for a counseling session that afternoon and explained that she needed to spend some time reflecting and praying". Choose something you do like this, and explain to the other that you need to spend "some time on your own". Avoid the temptation to say you have some other kindness to perform and ensure you get over that you need to look after yourself. How does this feel? Why?

2   Church Reformers 500 years ago railed against 'salvation by works' – the notion that God will save us and accept us if we do good things. Ask yourself the question: Why does it feel better to win someone's approval, rather than just freely receive it?

3   Make a list of ten people who are close to you. For each name, reflect on this: Does he/she give or take more from me? How many 'givers' are there? Are there more 'takers'?

4   Following on from exercise 3, reflect on a recent 'giving' action of one of your friends. How did it make you feel? Did you think something like, "I must pay them back in some way"?

5   Write down the first half of **1 John 4:10**: *this is love, not that we have loved God, but that He loved us.* What is it about God's love that is so different? Memorize these words and meditate on them frequently during the day.

6   Grace realized that God loved her: 'just as she had looked at her children when they were born and instantly adored them just as they were'. This suggests that parents' love is unconditional. Try to picture yourself in the loving arms of God, like a baby in a mother's arms. What does this feel like? Does it change your idea of love at all? If so, in what way?

Keith's Story: Type 1

... and the truth will set you free
John 8:32

Blessed is the man who finds wisdom...She is a tree of life to those who embrace her...
Proverbs 3:13–18

Keith opened the brass clasp on his wife's personal diary and started reading where it fell open:

> *Keith is so critical all the time. He makes me nervous in case I do something wrong. Today he watched me making dinner and cleaned up after me as I went. And then after dinner he didn't want to talk because he put the dishes in the dishwasher and tidied away everything. Nothing I do is ever good enough for him. I thought the dinner was really nice, and it took me ages to do it after a heavy day at the Centre, but his first comment was, "I prefer it with less salt."*

When Keith was eight, his father was stopped for speeding. The policeman approached the driver's window, which was wound down, and said: "What speed you were doing, sir?" "Oh, around 30 or so I think, officer..." came the reply, to which Keith responded from the back seat: "No, Dad, it was nearly 45. I could see from here!" As a child Keith had been such a fanatic for the truth that he would correct anyone he believed to be exaggerating, or simply not telling the truth, no matter what the social consequences.

Aged 28, he worked as an insurance sales manager, overseeing the work of 11 junior colleagues, mostly checking their paperwork and making up reports for the divisional manager. He was good at his job and enjoyed it. Keith's colleagues were full of admiration for his work ethic, for his honesty (what you see is what you get) and for amazing his work absence record – he had called in sick only twice in seven years. He was perhaps more admired than loved, but that was the way Keith preferred it: his motivation was knowing that he was helping to maintain decent standards at work.

At his local church Keith was a deacon. Brought up by his parents (whom he later started calling "nominal Christians") in a traditional Anglican church, he joined a Baptist church when he went away to university because, as he put it, "the Baptists are more committed than your typical C of E." He was baptized as a student, and explained to his parents that since a baby doesn't know what's happening to it, the Anglican christening he'd had wasn't the same as the deeply moving experience of baptism by immersion, which is also truer to Bible teaching.

While he was at university he met Grace. She was in the year ahead of him, studying to be a nurse. Keith loved her gentle, caring nature and he found her physically very attractive – like him, she was slim and not too tall. They decided early on that they would wait until they were married to have sex, even though many of their friends thought they were odd and old-fashioned. When they made comments about it, Keith would usually respond that he, as a Christian, had a very high view of sex and thought that it was so valuable it was worth waiting until they were married to experience it.

Yet the problem Grace and Keith had actually seemed to be all about sex: since their first child was born two years previously (a year or so after they were married) Grace 'let herself go' in Keith's eyes and she was also much less interested in sex. Keith felt both letdown and frustrated. They argued about it quite a lot: usually it came down to Keith complaining about Grace not losing a bit of weight and Grace explaining that she couldn't help "not feeling like it."

Keith did an Enneagram test a few weeks before and

discovered that he was a 1. He readily identified with the yearning for truth, doing the best possible job and striving for high standards. He also saw that on his bad days he was a rather critical and complaining person; that was something Grace had found hard to take on several occasions (she was a 2 and didn't like fault-finding one bit.) But that which Grace called "nagging" and "criticism" Keith called "telling the truth" – to which he sometimes added the biblical addendum "… *in a spirit of love.*" He wondered why she should be so reluctant to hear the truth, if by doing so she could put something right. Soon after completing the personality test he had been struck by something written in a book on the subject: "*If you are interested in transformation, no element is more important than developing a love of truth. The truth encompasses both our fearful reactions and the greater resources of our soul*" (*The Wisdom of the Enneagram*, p. 345). Keith certainly yearned for the truth!

He was greatly annoyed when he heard that the pastor's daughter had left her husband for another man, who happened to be a deacon in the same church. At the deacons' meeting Keith was amazed to note that nothing was being done to discipline the man, who was sitting there apparently unconcerned. (With what Keith described to his father as "bare-faced cheek". Typically, his father's response was: "Well, it could have been worse; she could've gone off with another woman!" Keith loved his father, but often found him flippant, annoying and frustrating.)

Immediately after the deacons' meeting, before he had even talked about it with Grace, he phoned the pastor to tell him what he thought – or rather, as he put it later to Grace, to "explain to him that he would support any measures the pastor thought fit to prevent the deacons' court being brought into disrepute."

It made Keith's blood boil when the pastor responded by referring to the Bible, and the woman caught in adultery and how Jesus had not condemned her. He knew he'd later regret it, but Keith couldn't stop himself saying, "But he at least told the woman to '*sin no more*'. **You** could try that!" The pastor pointed out that the deacon was unmarried, and that the guiltier party was really his own daughter, who was the married one.

By now Keith's anger was far from righteous, and he blurted out, "So is it OK for a deacon to commit adultery, as long as it's with your daughter?" The pastor paused, and quietly told Keith that he didn't want to discuss the matter further on the phone, and said goodbye.

Keith's convictions were difficult to argue with. He tried to live by high standards; he insisted that they buy fair-trade coffee, tea, sugar and chocolate and had persuaded the church to do the same. To Keith, the world was a broken and impure place and he was driven by a desire to clean it up and mend it. He had bought a hybrid eco-friendly car. On the issue of adultery he could demonstrate that Bible teaching was against it and the church he was part of made a point of upholding clear moral teaching like this. His integrity was usually very attractive and many of his friends shared his strong values, even though they were perhaps less successful in living them out.

After his outburst on the phone to the pastor, he wrote a letter resigning from both the diaconate and the church. Satisfied, he left it by the front door and went to bed. As he told Grace everything that had happened she listened in silence. She could see his point of view, but she was worried about the way he had spoken to the pastor. However, she knew better than to tell her husband what she actually thought.

By one of those strange coincidences that seem to happen too often to be mere coincidences, Keith's bible reading that night was **Philippians 3:1–14** about Paul's background. He began reading:

> *If someone else thinks they have reasons to put confidence in the flesh, I have more: circumcised on the eighth day, of the people of Israel, of the tribe of Benjamin, a Hebrew of*

*Hebrews; in regard to the law, a Pharisee; as for zeal, perse-
cuting the church; as for righteousness based on the law,
faultless.*

Keith paused and reflected on his own past and how he had often
felt it wasn't as 'pure' as some of his fellow Christians, who had
been brought up by missionaries in India, for example, or another
man he knew who had come to faith at the age of seven. He read
on:

*But whatever were gains to me I now consider loss... What is
more, I consider everything a loss... I consider them garbage,
that I may gain Christ and be found in him, not having a
righteousness of my own that comes from the law, but that
which is through faith in Christ – the righteousness that
comes from God on the basis of faith.*

With amazing speed – like those time-lapse films which show a
seed growing into a fully-grown plant in the course of a minute –
the thought occurred to Keith that he had been profoundly
wrong. It grew into a complete conviction before he realized it:
his convictions and principles – the fair-trade, his sexual purity,
even his adherence to Bible teachings – were to him like Paul's
"righteousness of my own". He had so long struggled to keep
stay faithful and true that he had neglected to see that goodness
and faith were gifts of God.

It was then that the awful notion struck him that he had been
unfair to the pastor. He hadn't even given him the chance to
explain. What if there were mitigating factors? Above all, who
was he, Keith, to stand in judgment of others – even if they have
committed adultery? With huge regret, he realized that he had
been the one to *"throw the first stone"*. He fervently prayed for
forgiveness as Grace snored lightly in the bed next to him and
decided to bin the letter he had earlier hurriedly written to the

pastor.

Grace got up early the next morning for her 7 am shift and as she opened the front door to go out she noticed the letter addressed to the pastor. Sensing an opportunity to help Keith out and save him a visit to the pastor's house (which she thought might result in further acrimony), she took it with her and resolved to drop it through the manse letterbox on her way to work. By the time Keith came downstairs an hour later the pastor had had a rather ugly early morning surprise.

Keith was livid that Grace had interfered. She didn't receive his early morning text until her break at 11, but when she heard that he had changed his mind about sending it, she felt all the worse for having aggravated, rather than improved, the situation.

As for Pastor Graham, the letter cemented his opinion that Keith was more principled than caring and by the end of the day he had written a very politely phrased note, regretting Keith's decision, but accepting it. He didn't write that he was glad enough that there would one fewer critical voice in the diaconate at a time when he was feeling the heat from his daughter's marital breakup. In the Baptist church circles Graham moved in even being the innocent victim in a divorce is frowned upon; it's letting the side down. Keith certainly thought so.

Even though just the night before he had resolved to "turn a new leaf" and stop standing in judgment of others, the added pressure now made it doubly difficult for Keith to do what, in his heart of hearts, he knew he should: admit his mistake and apologize. It was no longer just a question of asking the pastor to forgive him getting angry on the phone; he also would need to retract his letter and look a fool in front of his wife, admitting that she had been right. Suddenly it seemed much easier to revert to a more familiar strategy: point the finger of blame at others.

Despite the impact of his evening bible reading (or maybe

partly because of it) he found that he was becoming more and more judgmental and critical of others, and during the heated argument he and Grace fell into after coming home from work, heard himself saying: "Why is everyone so devious and deceitful?" He was unable to see that his wife's actions were motivated by concern and a desire to help; the pastor simply seemed to be weak and devoid of backbone. To admit his mistakes would have required him to accept that he too was imperfect and flawed; he was so stressed out he couldn't manage something so demanding – however right it was to do it.

It turned out that the pastor's daughter had not left her husband; she had been left by her husband. She had turned for help to the deacon, who was an old school friend. They had met twice. There had been no impropriety in their relationship, even by Keith's exacting standards. Even the pastor had believed the gossip about them; or rather, he had feared that it would be true and so he had acted as if it was.

A few days later, after church, Keith told the pastor how sorry he was for his behavior. "Let's think no more about it," the pastor responded, in his tolerant and gentle way. "I would like you back on the diaconate, though."

"I couldn't…" Keith stammered. "I'm so embarrassed about what people will think. I must appear like a complete imbecile!"

"Only the church secretary knows about your letter. I can explain that it was all a misunderstanding."

"I really don't feel good enough to be a deacon," Keith admitted, glumly.

"And who is ever good enough to serve God?"

A year or so later Grace was away for three days with the young women's group, which she led. As Keith tidied the bedroom after coming home from work – her absence meant that he could do this without hearing her complain about it – he noticed Grace's diary on the bedside cabinet. She sometimes spoke about her "spiritual journal" which she had started some years before, but Keith rarely saw it, and still less frequently saw her writing it. He presumed that she had meant to take it with her on the weekend away, but had instead left it behind.

As he opened it, clicking apart the brass buckle that kept it shut, he knew that what he was doing was deeply wrong. He justified it to himself by saying that he merely wanted to understand her better and improve their relationship. Whatever his intent, what he read transfixed him.

Keith is so critical all the time. He makes me nervous in case I do something wrong. Today he watched me making dinner and cleaned up after me as I went. And then after dinner he didn't want to talk because he put the dishes in the dishwasher and tidied away everything. Nothing I do is ever good enough for him. I thought the dinner was really nice, and it took me ages to do it after a heavy day at the Centre, but his first comment was, "I prefer it with less salt."

When we went to bed I could feel him watching me get undressed. But when I looked round I could see that it wasn't that he fancied me, but that he was noticing the weight I have put on. It's not a lot, but most of my clothes are a bit tighter now than they were when I got them.

I know he's really idealistic and I admire him for sticking to his principles, but sometimes it seems that he only loves me if I'm good enough to be loved. It's like I have to meet his standards all the time. If I don't, he's really cold with me. Sometimes he doesn't say what's wrong, but I know that I've let him down. He seems to be getting worse.

He went on the other night about the women's group. I don't know if he's jealous that I have set this thing up, but he started up again about how five of them aren't "saved" and that I should lay it on the line about what God expects of them. I would really like to introduce him to them, maybe even get him to come along and give a talk, but I'm worried that he'll upset them by being too religious and demanding.

Her words cut him to the very core. At first, he felt angry at being so criticized, but soon his anger subsided into hurt. That evening it took him a long time to fall asleep, as a storm of thoughts went through his head. It even occurred to him that they would separate. Finally he drifted off into sleep, but his rest was disturbed by fierce dreams that troubled him, so that when he awoke he was tired and irritable. He forced himself to pray over breakfast, much more out of duty than desire. Momentarily he felt better inside, but quickly he felt judged and worthless. He wished he had work to go to; Saturdays were long without Grace. He thought about collecting Elisa from his in-laws, but quickly dismissed the idea – they would be very disappointed to miss out on their first long weekend with their beloved and so far only grandchild.

He sat staring out of the window. *"Sometimes it seems that he only loves me if I'm good enough to be loved..."* He would find it easier to accept if she weren't partly right: he had himself reflected how much easier it was for him to love people who behaved well. But he knew that he couldn't admit that he had found her journal and read it; he knew what the brass-buckled book was and how personal it was to her: to have opened it was, in Grace's eyes, like a violation of her deepest privacy. Even to Keith it was a violation: he felt sullied by the criticism of him which it contained: it was like one of Elisa's stinking nappies thrown into the clean wardrobe of his life.

It was then he resolved two things: to fast until Grace returned and to clean the house from top to bottom.

Cleaning things was for Keith like a workaday sacrament: it did him good to think he was being useful and cleaning things was for him like a cherished symbol. He pulled Elisa's chest of drawers away from the wall and a thick line of dust was revealed on the floor and another on the skirting board: "Grace never bothers what it's really like," he thought. "It just needs to look OK." He pulled the mattress of her small bed and upended it against the wall and then did the same with the base. The clots and clusters of dust swirled around as if annoyed they had been discovered and disturbed. "We are finding out the dirt this weekend," he muttered. He attacked the dirt with the vacuum cleaner – the new hypoallergenic one which he had bought for Grace's birthday. It was full by the time Elisa's room was finished.

He sensed that the room wasn't clean enough. He trudged downstairs and fetched the bleach and a sponge. Carefully he wiped the skirting board with bleach from behind the door all the way round the room, pulling the bed away from the wall again. He re-soaked the sponge with bleach and did the rest of the room. The stark, bitter smell of the bleach satisfied him like a punishment.

And so it went on. Their own room was a disgrace: a great thick blanket of dust coated the back of their wardrobe; the bed hadn't been moved in years; the bedside cabinets hid wodges of dirt that he sucked away with energy and purpose. He needed to empty the cleaner halfway through and he had to change the filter also. The spare room was a little less disgusting; he had decorated it not long before, but still there were several areas which needed thorough cleaning.

He stopped at a few minutes before three, went downstairs and took a glass of cold water. He wouldn't wash either, he decided, until an hour or so before Grace's return: he needed to prove to himself – and of course to God – that he was serious. Before he resumed work, he opened all the windows wide. There was a stiff breeze and it blew pleasingly through the house.

When he had finished the living room it was a little after nine at night and it was dark. His stomach rumbled painfully. He was pleased with the pain; it proved his commitment. He permitted himself a second glass of water. He had decided to spend the rest of the day reading the Bible. It took his mind off his hunger to read it and he loved the rich ornateness of the King James

Version. When he was reading religiously like this, he always used the old Bible; it added a grandeur and sense of occasion to his reading. Once he had heard about the Greek Orthodox Church using a cleansed version of the Greek language in their liturgies, unsullied by everyday usage and lower thoughts. The KJV reminded him pleasingly of this. When he had finished reading Genesis he looked up from the armchair and noticed the back of the TV, coated with a thick smear of dust. He had turned it so that it faced the wall but hadn't noticed the back. He got up, fetched a large cloth and a wet sponge and cleaned it.

As he rinsed the sponge and cloth in hot water he felt his stomach again. It was a pleasure to deny himself in this way. He had cleaned the house, fasted since breakfast and had hardly given a thought to the entry in Grace's diary. He decided to read Exodus and then go to bed. He went through to the living room, knelt on the floor and started reading. By the time Moses had seen the burning bush his knees were stinging with pain from the hard wooden floor. When Aaron's stick became a snake, they were almost numb, but his back, sore from the day's bending and straightening, was now sending sharp signals of complaint. He sensed the need to subdue these aches and pains and sublimate them by devotion. When the locusts plagued the Pharaoh, he felt the whole of his right side stiffen with pain as if a disc were about to slip. He straightened his back and resumed his reading. The French windows were still open and he noticed his neighbor glancing over the hedge at him. It would do no harm for the man to see him like this, he reflected. When the first Passover came, Keith sensed that he was being told to sit in a chair.

Relieved, he sank back into the armchair, closed his eyes to pray and fell asleep.

He awoke with a sour taste in his mouth and the cold evening air filling the room. The light from the living room spilled out onto his lawn. He closed the doors and switched off the light. In a half-sleep he closed the downstairs windows and locked the front door. He trudged slowly up the stairs into the darkness of the landing. He denied himself the pleasure of lighting his way to the bedroom, feeling his way into the bedroom. The strong smell reminded him of a swimming pool. He fell onto the bed and almost immediately was asleep.

He awoke with the sun shining onto a corner of the bedroom rug and the wind chilling him slightly. He looked at the alarm clock and realized he had only a few minutes to get ready for church. He would go to the Fellowship; he had decided that it would be more appropriate. He changed his clothes and dabbed some aftershave around his neck to cover the smell of sweat. He was hungrier than he had been for years: the fasting and the physical effort together were a punishment which almost made him smile with joy.

It was when Sarah waved her arm in the air to identify herself as the counselor during the welcomes soon after the start of the service that Keith realized whom he was sitting next to. He had heard about her florid history from gossip at work, but had never met her. Strangely enough he noticed that she smelt strongly of Pastor Graham. It couldn't be that she used the same scent…

After the service he introduced himself to her and noticed that she blanched when he mentioned that he was from the Baptist church. At work sometimes people reacted in a similar way.

"Oh, the Baptist church?" she said. Keith noticed that her teeth were almost perfectly aligned and her lips pouted pleasantly when she said "church". "So how are things there?"

"Oh, yes, well fine actually. Pastor Graham's doing a good job. D'you know him… at all?"

Sarah looked away. Keith imagined that she had seen someone whom she recognized. "Yes, we have met. Charming man, great preacher I believe; I've only heard him the once."

There was a pause. Keith found his breathing had become

shallow and he found it difficult to look away from this beautiful girl next to him. He searched for something to say, but nothing would come. Their eyes met; she was clearly expecting him to speak.

"In fact... it's silly... you'll know all about this from your counseling no doubt, but I felt quite guilty coming here. And er..." he was stumbling on, not knowing where he was going, "The strange thing is that your scent reminded me of Pastor Graham. Guilt is a strange thing."

Sarah went from pale to bright red in a moment. She turned away and seemed to have seen the person she had recognized earlier. "Must go and see..." she began and then she was gone, leaving Keith blushing in his seat, wondering if he had said something wrong.

When Grace returned, to a pristine if decidedly bleachy house, Keith said nothing. He had mulled it over repeatedly but had come to the same conclusion: saying anything would reveal that he had violated her privacy and he couldn't admit to doing that. He had punished himself for doing it, by fasting for a day and a half and by cleaning the house, but making it up to Grace was a different matter: his integrity and honesty were his strongest suits with her. Half an hour after Grace's return her parents arrived with Elisa, fast asleep in her grandfather's arms. The four of them sat for an hour chitchatting idly until her parents left.

Grace was calm and relaxed after the 3-day retreat with her women friends. It had been a success: everyone reported that it had been "very nice" and "a place of real love" where relationships had grown. Keith smiled approvingly and told his wife how well she had done and how important her work was. When they went to bed she fell asleep very quickly, but Keith stared at his bible reading booklet with a bitter and hungry taste in his mouth until he finally fell asleep sitting up with his head over to one side.

At work the next day he tried to avoid speaking to people. He had eaten four pieces of toast ravenously at breakfast while Grace played with Elisa in the living room. He was still hungry but refused to give in to the temptation to eat more. Harry was talking with someone about some gossip about the pastor Graham. As he strained to listen he reflected that unbelievers will invent all manner of stories to denigrate Christian faith and the church. As Harry got up to leave he heard him say: "But she's less than half his age! Lucky man!"

During the afternoon he prepared himself for Grace. He decided that he would try to let her know that he was making changes in his personal life – but without giving her even an inkling of the reason why. He would tell her that the sermon at the Fellowship had really spoken to him, although in truth he could scarcely remember what it had been about.

Once Elisa was in bed he prepared a cup of coffee for his wife as he usually did. "Great message at the Fellowship yesterday. Really spoke to me..." he began.

"Oh you were there were you? What was the sermon about?"

"You know... I can hardly remember the theme, 'cos it just got right to me. Made me realize how critical I can be..." Grace nodded sympathetically and did that half-smile which he disliked so much. He went on: "It's like that Enneagram stuff says: when you're under stress you move away from the good things about your type and you move towards the bad stuff." ·

Grace disliked hearing him speak about the Enneagram. She thought it too analytical and weird with its talk about fears and superego messages. But if it was helping Keith see how judgmental he could be, she thought, then maybe it would work for him.

"When I'm on top of my game I can be idealistic and positive, but I know that I can also be critical and..." he hesitated, not wanting to repeat the word "demanding" which had stuck in his memory from reading it in her diary. "...and so judgmental."

It was at this point that he expected her to comfort him and tell him that he wasn't so critical and judgmental. When she didn't, he started feeling anger welling up inside. Then she said, "Maybe you should think about going to see the counselor at the Fellowship... Sarah I think she's called. One of the ladies has been to her and she said she was very good."

"That's strange," Keith responded, forgetting his anger now, "I happened to be sitting next to her yesterday. I had no idea who she was. That's a coincidence."

"You know what Graham calls 'coincidences' – 'God-incidents'. Maybe God was telling you something."

When Keith arrived for his first appointment with Sarah ten days later, she stared at him as if he was her nemesis. She recognized him instantly: this was the man who had pointed out that she smelled of Graham. He must know. Her immediate thought was that as Graham had been approached by Brian Cannon so she was now being approached by this man, whoever he was. She just knew he went to the Baptist church. She nervously and tentatively shook his hand and waved him to a seat in the counseling room.

"It was such a coincidence to be sitting next to you that Sunday I came along... " Keith began, trying to break the ice. Sarah was unable to speak. She nodded, her whole body rocking slightly. "But as Graham says, coincidences are usually God-incidents," he affirmed, smiling. To Sarah his smile was snakelike. He looked so trim, neat and hard, his eyes peering at her with their owl-like keenness through his glasses – which looked as if he machine-polished them every five minutes. She managed to smile in the way someone will do to pre-empt an attack, a smile that said "Be nice to me, please!" He had come straight to the point, anyway. She nodded, trying to look at him with her "Please go on!" look because she couldn't speak, not coherently anyway. She was too afraid.

Keith blundered on, deciding that she wanted him to outline his situation. "I guess you can keep things hidden from others for long enough, but there comes a point when it's important to come clean, look for forgiveness and… well, change things."

Sarah was close to tears. So he knew, but how? Maybe he was a friend of Brian Cannon's and he had been sent to sort her out as Brian had done with Graham. As Keith looked at her beautiful face, he found her very easy to talk to. She seemed so open, kind and pure. The pain in her face reflected his own hurt and he went on: "I mean, when things threaten a marriage and family and ministry, then it just needs to stop." A high-pitched squeak was emitted from Sarah's throat, together with the words, "I agree." She realized that it had to stop. The thought of even seeing Graham again seemed a lifetime and worlds away.

Keith's eyes softened with tears as he looked at Sarah: she was such a good counselor! He could sense her empathy with his pain; it even seemed as if she was about to cry. He got up and by some strange instinct put his hand on her head. He intended it to be comforting.

As Sarah felt his hand, the thought occurred to her that he was taking aim to slap her, hard, across her face for being such a devious, corrupting harlot with Graham. When he didn't, but instead sat down again she was puzzled – so puzzled, in fact, that she looked up at stared at Keith with a quizzical look on her face.

"Sorry. You looked so… you don't need to cry for **me**!" Now she was completely bemused. She was blinking and trying to do that smile thing she had tried to perfect. "The thing is, the only reason I know what I know is that I read it somewhere I really shouldn't have been looking, so I'm a bit ashamed."

"Oh," she responded. Where on earth could he have read about them? Had Graham been keeping a journal of some kind?

"But I know the score and I'm determined that it's going to stop. I've prayed and fasted about it and I've made my promise to God. Insofar as it's in my power, it's over."

Then the thought that she would never see Graham again

washed like a dark shroud over Sarah, filling her sensitive heart with such sadness that she gave up all pretense of composure and burst into tears – inconsolable tears of grief, pain and passion. Her weeping had stopped Keith from talking, at least: he was staring at her with an expression of utter powerlessness and incomprehension. Her head fell into her lap and her whole body was riven with shakes and shiverings as the crying went on and on. After a few moments she heard the door open and then close and when she opened her bleary red eyes he was gone.

Keith was nearly sixty and his neatly-cut hair was entirely grey before he found peace and harmony within himself. For many years he had walked his own Damascus road without encountering any life-changing visions or hearing a voice that would bring him up short and turn his life around. He had some years ago started training himself to hear himself, really hear himself when he judged people and complained about others' and his own failings. He knew very well that his striving for perfection was a pale and broken shadow of God's true perfection. And now slowly, without any drama or fanfare, he found himself relaxing and letting go of his rather sad attempts at self-betterment. His heart was at last open to receive – a heart which had since childhood been shut tight until he could be persuaded it deserved to be blessed. Now, still far from perfect but with no striving or struggle, he was at peace with the One who alone could grant him wholeness and purity.

Spiritual Exercises for 1s

1   As a child – and as an adult – Keith was "such a fanatic for the truth" that he lost friends through it. Can you identify times when like Keith you were "more principled than caring"?

2   What difference might it make to you if, in instead of just telling the truth, you tried *speaking the truth in love*? (**Ephesians 4:15**) Can you think of some examples from your own experience and behavior?

3   Spend a day observing the critical spirit inside you making his presence known. Don't judge, repress or condemn; just observe.

4   You may be your own fiercest critic, which means that God is not. If God accepts you and loves you as you are, why can't you? Pray about this and reflect on Jesus' words in the woman caught in adultery incident Keith alludes to in this story: *neither do I condemn you.*

5   The apostle Paul yearned to *gain Christ* which meant *"not having a righteousness of my own"* (**Philippians 3:8–9**). This was a big sacrifice for Paul; are you prepared to make it?

6   Make a diary of your own critical comments and judgments over a one week period. Be as honest as you can. Review it two weeks later: are there patterns to be observed? Do you tend to be strongest with people closest to you, or less well-known?

7   For one day, ensure you make two positive comments for every negative one. Don't make up naïve comments; be genuinely grateful. Try doing this for two days, then three and so on. Increase the ratio from two to one to three, and then four to one.

8   At the start of each day and at least twice during the day, spend five minutes noting things which are good, right

and happy about your world. Write them in an e-mail or text to yourself.

Graham's Story: Type 3

What good will it be for someone to gain the whole world, yet forfeit their soul? Or what can anyone give in exchange for their soul?
Matthew 16:26

The LORD does not look at the things people look at. People look at the outward appearance, but the LORD looks at the heart.
1 Samuel 16:7

As he stood at the front of the church delivering his message in his relaxed style Graham told himself he hadn't felt so good in years. He scanned the faces of the congregation and observed that there were several who were openly admiring – Mrs. Harper, Bob Hanson and Sarah Brown – and many more who clearly approved of what he was preaching about judgmentalism. Keith Simpson looked stony-faced, as if he felt the sermon was directed at him, which perhaps it was. Above all, Graham sensed his acceptance by God and he even momentarily imagined the Lord also nodding his approval.

Under Pastor Graham's leadership the church had seen significant growth. For a start, two old stalwarts who had been thorns in the side for years had stopped attending, one due to declining health and the other because she had started to feel isolated in her critical position: it was an isolation that Graham had skillfully and actually quite lovingly pointed out to her. Then the congregation had grown significantly, largely due to members bringing friends, neighbors and family along to see the 'new' man at the Baptist church – tall, slim, rather handsome and very well turned-out Graham McCreadie. He also spoke very well, with a gentle Scottish accent and with an obvious attention to detail in the words and expressions he used. He was the first pastor of that church to write out his sermons in full – not that you would know it, as his delivery was conversational and exquisitely polished.

Tim, one of the deacons, noticed a further change which was more subtle – the improvement in standards of dress. Tim's unconcern about his own appearance was legendary, but within three or four months it was also much more obvious as most of the congregation made an extra effort to appear as neat and smart as Pastor Graham. He had that effect on most people, inspiring both confidence and emulation. And yet, even after two years of Graham's ministry, very few people in the church really knew him well. Although he was able to speak with people about their innermost worries and their fears, he would virtually never speak about his own even to family and close friends.

Once, his wife Anne had asked him about this. "Y'know, I'm really not that interested in myself," he replied. "I would say it's a bit vain to be too self-aware, and there's something humble about someone who doesn't go on about his own feelings. Besides, didn't Jesus say we had to forget about ourselves and carry his cross?"

Anne could tell by his long answer that she had hit a nerve.

Anne had often felt jealous of Graham's easy rapport with their daughter Catherine as she grew up, whereas she had always felt a bit distant from her. Sometimes she actually felt she almost excluded. At these times she most resented Graham's apparent closeness with her. What enraged her was Graham's tolerance of Catherine's wilder excesses: he would never tell her that she had gone too far; that was always left to Anne and even then Graham rarely expressed open support of his wife. Anne would tell herself angrily that Graham valued Catherine's friendship and approval more than he should, and as a result the girl was growing up without a "steady moral rudder" as Anne's sister once called it.

After one particularly annoying episode, when Catherine had argued with the school head teacher and written to the local paper about it, Anne resolved to try to get to the root of the problem with Graham.

"Were your own parents really lax with you?" she asked, trying to keep her tone neutral.

"Lax, no," he replied. "But I don't think I'm lax with Katie. She has lots of energy and – "

"And so she needs to know when and where she can let go of it. Shouting at the head teacher and then writing a letter of complaint to the paper is not appropriate for a 14 year old daughter of a pastor."

There was silence, during which Graham hoped his wife would drop the matter. Then she remembered that she had wanted to get him to speak about his own childhood.

"So did you do everything your parents told you to do?" she asked.

"Pretty much. My mum was a demanding type I suppose. Nothing I did was ever good enough, even when I won prizes at school and got 'A's' in my exams. Maybe that's why I don't want Katie to feel she's let us down. I hated feeling that."

They had been married over 15 years and this was more than Graham had ever said to her about his childhood. She recalled Graham's mother speaking about his first nativity play, aged three, when at the end in the silence that followed the applause, Graham's voice had rung out in the church: "Was I good, Mum?" and everyone had laughed. Graham left the room and Anne realized, in rare moment of profound insight, that her husband actually had a low sense of his own worth. That was why he sought everyone's approval. He wasn't showing off (as his critics sometimes complained); he was looking for affirmation.

Graham had come to the Baptist church with a near-perfect pedigree: brought up in a Christian home, Head Boy at secondary school, first class honors in theology, married while still at university, best preacher of his year and winner of all three class medals in biblical knowledge. He had then spent a year in an American Baptist seminary, where he had impressed people so much that rumor had it he had been offered positions in four churches. On his return home he had worked for several years in an inner-city church, where their daughter Catherine had been born. On top of all this, he was an able pianist and played five-a-side football twice a week. He was surely the ideal pastor.

After church that Sunday, he could hear conversations buzzing about the topic of his sermon. The fact that his own daughter was involved added an edge to the issue that worked largely in his favor. Although she had a reputation of being a bit wild, word around the church had it that she had suffered as a young child in the inner-city area where she had been born and this explained some of her behavior.

The deacons' court the following week turned out to be something of a trial. Not that anyone said anything during the meeting itself, but Keith was evidently very worked up and Tim was sitting a few seats away from him, apparently blissfully unaware that several other deacons believed he had committed adultery with the pastor's daughter. A few minutes after Graham had gotten home and heaved a sigh of relief that it was over, the phone rang. Before he could indicate to Anne that he wasn't available, he heard her say that the pastor had just that minute gotten in and she would fetch him.

It was Keith, telling him that Tim should have been disciplined at the deacons' court. Since Pastor Graham didn't know the full details of what had happened between Catherine and Tim, he couldn't categorically say that he was innocent. But what got to him with Keith's verbal assault was his anger; in fact as Keith berated the pastor for his moral laxity Graham caught himself wondering why he never got angry like this about the moral failings of others. Maybe it was a shortcoming. Then there was a silence and he realized that Keith was waiting for him to respond.

The words were out of his mouth before he realized what they implied: *"You know, Jesus himself refused to judge or reject the woman caught in adultery."* Once he had uttered them, he realized that Keith would take this as confirmation that Catherine had committed adultery – obviously! Keith's anger stepped up a notch with his next comment, and Graham managed to quietly say that he didn't wish to discuss the matter further on the phone.

He put the receiver down and went through to his study. He sat for several minutes contemplating the situation and trying to work out a solution. He could hardly ask his daughter point-blank whether she had slept with geeky Tim. Surely not... but then he recalled several occasions when he had noticed Tim eyeing up Catherine in a way that Keith, for one, would have labeled "lustful". Could it be that she had sought refuge in his friendship and then they had... It would be none of his business if it was anyone but Tim. But then if something untoward had happened, surely Tim wouldn't have been able to sit there so cool and calm at the deacons' court as if butter wouldn't melt in his mouth? On the other hand, the only person Graham knew who could carry off that kind of barefaced cheek was Tim, with his air of detachment and unworldliness.

And as he was praying, heaven was opened and the Holy Spirit descended on him in bodily form like a dove. And a voice came from heaven: "You are my Son, whom I love; with you I am well pleased."
Luke 3:21–2

When a letter arrived the next day, delivered by hand well before the normal post, Pastor Graham had a strong inkling of its contents.

Dear Graham,

I think you know that I have been loyal and supportive of your ministry and therefore it is not as a personal attack that I write today.

My concern is for the integrity, standing and reputation of the diaconate. I cannot condone the toleration of a sinful deacon, or one who appears to be acting in a way to bring us into disrepute.

I therefore resign with immediate effect from the diaconate and church membership.

Yours,

Keith

Even though he had half expected it, Graham was disappointed and hurt by the letter. He didn't like feeling rejected by anyone, even someone whose departure would make life easier for him. He had long felt that Keith's principles were stronger than his human compassion – a man of the head but not of the heart.

Shortly after finishing his breakfast, he received a text message from Catherine. She usually texted before phoning for a private conversation so that she avoided speaking with her mother. He slipped unnoticed into his study and phoned her.

"Hey, Dad!" Catherine sounded buoyant. "I guess you heard about me and Sandy… ?"

"I heard rumors…"

"It's true. He left last week."

"And you waited all this time to tell me?"

"I thought he might come back," she lied. "He does love his dramatic gestures."

"Has he gone off with that… er Martine?"

"Nadine, yes. She wants to have his babies."

"And you don't?"

"Yuck, Dad, how could you? Imagine another little Sandy-let in the world!"

"So how are you then? Are you at work at the moment?"

"I had a couple of days off to get myself together, but I'm OK. It feels more honest now he's gone." There was a pause, and then she added: "Will you tell Mum?"

"It would be better if you told her yourself..." her father replied.

"I know, but I don't really feel up to it. She loves Sandy. He can do no wrong in her eyes. I'm sure she'll think I must've been a horrendous wife or he wouldn't have left."

"Then you can tell her the truth so that she gets the right idea," Graham replied.

"Please, Dad? I will speak about it to her, but give me a few days... ?"

"Well I can't force you to speak with her... and if you don't then I'll have to."

There was another pause, after which Graham asked: "And there are rumors about you and Tim..."

"Tim? I've seen him a couple of times, but just for a chat. We're not dating or anything. We've known each other for years."

"And I know the way he looks at you..."

"Oh, protective Dad! You're so sweet!"

"Yeah, yeah... but even if there's nothing in it for you, I'm sure he wants it to be his way. He'll see this as his opportunity."

"I can report that he has done nothing inappropriate and nothing that merits reporting to the diaconate!"

Although she was speaking jokingly about it, Graham was hugely relieved. Once their conversation had ended, he wrote a note to Keith regretting his decision to resign, but accepting it. It was just after nine. He would post the letter through Keith's door during his afternoon visits.

The big old clock that had belonged to her grandmother rang the half hour. It was half past two. Anne watched as he left the house and drove off in their smart grey saloon car. She would have been astounded and shocked if she had been able to see where her husband went and what he then did, on that day of all days.

They hadn't spoken in three days. It started soon after the sermon; Anne hadn't known at the time about Catherine's marital breakdown and when someone at church had spoken about it, she felt very foolish. She accused Graham of keeping secrets; but she sensed that the real reason was that he didn't want to admit that his 'perfect' daughter had done something wrong – and right under his nose with one of his favorite deacons! His response – that he didn't want to discuss what he believed to be pure gossip – wasn't good enough for Anne and she had refused to talk to him until he apologized. He suggested that she could easily phone their daughter to find out the truth.

Graham had never got on with Sandy, Catherine's husband, so his departure now confirmed the pastor in his belief that he was the wrong man for his daughter. Sandy had never hidden his contempt for religious people in general and Christians in particular. He was a sentimental and emotional person, something that Graham found difficult to handle; he didn't believe Sandy was sincere. To make it worse, Anne loved Sandy like a son and sided with him when Sandy and Catherine had arguments, which, after the first six months or so of their marriage, was fairly frequently. The fact that he had grown his father's double-glazing firm into a multi-million pound a year turnover company didn't impress Graham at all. So when he heard rumors that Sandy and Catherine had split up, he resolved to say nothing until Catherine spoke to him about it.

After writing his brief note to Keith he went through to the lounge, where his wife was reading a book.

"That was Catherine on the phone. Sandy's left her for Nadine. Seems he had been nagging her to have kids and she refused. She's not ready. So he's gone and left her. And the rumors about her and Tim are nonsense. Might be good if you phoned her…"

His wife said nothing, but pretended to go back to her book, her jaws clenched tight shut. She refused to admit she had been wrong.

He worked in his study until lunch, which, for the third day running, he had prepared himself and eaten alone. He wrote an article for the church magazine and, as the old hallway clock indicated it was nearly two-thirty, he left the house and drove off in their smart grey car.

Since her husband had been arrested and sent to prison, Sarah had kept a low profile. After a few months she sued for divorce and began using her maiden name again. She led the counseling service in the Fellowship and was surprised one day to receive a phone call from Pastor Graham, asking for a private counseling session away from the Fellowship building, as he didn't want to be recognized. They had met twice at a coffee shop some miles away and he had talked about his marital problems, but on this occasion they had arranged for Graham to visit her at home.

Sarah was watching from the window as Graham's silver car parked a little distance down the other side of the road. She watched as he bought a ticket from the machine and almost said out loud "I hope he has enough money..."

She had left the door open and Graham came in to find Sarah in her dressing gown sitting on the sofa.

"Oh, I'm so sorry, Sarah. I didn't realize you weren't well... Shall I come back another day?"

"I'm not ill. I er..."

Immediately Graham understood. He recalled how awkward she had seemed when she suggested that they meet at her flat. She was standing up now, walking slowly towards him and looking at him with a steady gaze. He had just enough time to feel how wonderful it was to be openly admired by a young and beautiful woman before her lips touched his.

Two hours later Graham looked at Sarah as he lay beside her in the bed. She seemed to be asleep. He was dazed by the awful wonderfulness of what he had just done. "I need to get the car before I get a ticket," he said, getting up to dress. Sarah opened her eyes and smiled at him. Graham smiled back in his usual relaxed way, but had the tingling and tense feeling of having crossed a very wide and dangerous Rubicon.

As he drove home he couldn't stop thinking about Sarah – or rather, feeling about her, because the overwhelming sensation he had was of value – being held in high esteem by someone who really mattered.

It had been years since he and Anne had made love and during those years he had grown used to a marriage which was little more than a habit. She seemed to Graham sometimes like an unpaid tenant, living her own life, sharing nothing personal with him and showing little interest in him. Indeed she sometimes openly mocked his concern for what others said about him. As the stress at church grew, culminating in the fiasco around Catherine's marital problems and alleged dalliance with Tim, so did Graham's need for reassurance, admiration and support, but Anne was singularly unwilling – or unable – to give him any of these things.

When he looked at himself in the mirror as he waited at the traffic lights near their home, he looked and felt wonderful. The moral darkness of what he had done was blotted out by the blinding thrill of Sarah's gorgeous regard.

Because Anne hardly spoke to him and slept in a different bedroom, the signals which would usually alert a wife to her husband's infidelity passed her by. Once or twice over the years she had wondered if he would be unfaithful, but she had dismissed the idea as too far-fetched. He would surely do nothing to risk his reputation; he wasn't a brave man. Graham knew that his wife had a reasonably accurate grasp of his character and he resented it. To not be esteemed by the one who knew you best was, for Graham, both hurtful and insulting. What Anne did not realized – and neither, until this point, did Graham

– was the extent to which he could be deceitful in pursuit of his goals and indeed his desires.

It was in truth desire which impelled him to call on Sarah once again on the Saturday evening, after he had done the home visits he needed to do. In fact, as he listened to Mrs. Harper droning on about how much she had loved his sermon on judgmentalism and how the events had panned out to confirm the wisdom and timeliness of his message – of course she knew that Catherine and Tim were just friends – he could hardly get Sarah out of his mind's eye. While pooh-poohing the very notion that his daughter could do anything untoward with a deacon, here he was burning with desire for a young woman who was only his daughter's age.

He had to go on to see Gordon Skinner, the church secretary and frequent tormentor-in-chief. He was annoyed about the mini-scandal-that-never-was as he put it.

"It should have been nipped in the bud before it became a topic of idle conversation and more," he went on.

"Yes, I agree that it would have been better if that had been possible, Gordon." Graham often found himself being very firm and professional with Gordon Skinner, rather than charming and smooth as he was with most people in the church. "But the issue here is also about whether people have the right to meet together without silly people accusing them of… misbehavior." Graham stopped and imagined for one dreadful moment what Gordon would be saying if he knew about him and Sarah two days previously. "Misbehavior" echoed around his brain a little too long.

Gordon was irritated by Graham's words. *Silly people?* He had been one of them. He had long had his suspicions about Catherine and he didn't like Tim's quietness and stand-on-the-sidelines attitude. He liked to know what people thought and whether they were with him so he found Tim an irritant.

"The church – by that I mean The Church," – as he said this wagged his fingers in the air indicating quotation marks – "is like justice: it needs to be pure and honest but it also needs to be seen to be pure and honest. I can hardly believe that Catherine didn't know that her actions would be interpreted in the way they were."

Graham boiled inside: he couldn't stand people criticizing Catherine, least of all this annoying little man. But in a moment of lucidity he found a riposte that hid his anger beautifully: "Gordon, her husband has just left her. She is hurting and needs support. I don't think we should criticize church members for seeking support from our deacons. That's what they're there for."

Taken aback, Gordon took a mental step back. "Of course I understand, I do. I didn't mean to be critical. Maybe it's Tim who should've been more discrete about where and how he met Catherine…"

"And reject a call for help from an old friend and sister in the faith? This is no time for finger-pointing. Tim knew Catherine at school; he had no reason to believe anyone would suspect anything untoward. Rather than blame the people involved – the girl whose husband has walked out on her and the guy who was just wanting to help – we should be talking about the idle gossips who created the story out of nothing." Graham felt like adding, "Game, set and match!" He knew he had won the argument from the way Gordon was looking down now, nodding.

"Listen, I'm sorry, Gordon, but I need to go…"

"Yes, of course, thanks for dropping by. I think you're right." Gordon was relieved that the pastor was about to leave. He was far too clever for his own good sometimes, he reflected. When he shook his hand it was like you do at the end of a football game you've just lost.

Graham swung into his car with a lightness of step that he hadn't known for some years; adrenaline and testosterone seemed to be flowing in equal parts. It was nearly eight o'clock. He told himself that needed to be home by 10:30 or Anne might ask questions; before 10:15 she would hardly even notice.

As he drove towards the town center and Sarah's flat, he was aware that he was doing something wrong. His heart wasn't so dark that he could simply excuse himself for so immoral a deed. The first time, she had seduced him: he had gone there totally innocently and she had used her... well, her gorgeousness to overcome his resistance – not that he had put up much resistance, but really, how could a man resist such beauty? She had very clearly and firmly led that first step. But this time was quite different and he well knew that morally it was definitely not the same; it was he who was taking the initiative and making the first move. (For all he knew she might resist him this time!) A Latin motto sprang into his mind: *errare humanum est; persevere diabolicum.* [To err is human; to persist is of the devil.] He would have been forgiven the first indiscretion; if he had gone to the deacons and told them everything – everything – then he would have been recognized for his honesty and applauded for his integrity in coming to them.

But, he told himself, *c'est plus fort que moi* as the French say: it's stronger than me; I can't help myself. He could no more resist Sarah than a heroin user can easily give up his drug when it's sitting there in front of him. It's one thing to give up an addiction when you have to steal first to get money and then go buy it from a dealer; but when the supply is right there in front of your nose... who would blame you for just getting your fix? Sarah was so totally available and so... fulfilling!

It was not a sophisticated excuse, but in Graham's weakened state it was enough. Had his marriage been a happier one; had Catherine not just split up with Sandy; had Sarah not been so utterly gorgeous, then well, maybe he would have been driving away from Sarah's flat rather than towards it. He parked his car in as shaded a spot as possible and almost ran down the road towards Sarah's front door.

Anne brought Graham a cup of tea in bed the next morning. He was amazed. She hadn't done this in years; it would be a peace offering, an admission that she had been too harsh on him regarding Catherine. And she wouldn't want to still be cold-shouldering him at church, as people would see that and might ask questions. But he was pleased nonetheless.

"Late in last night?" she asked, happily, as if there had never been a problem between them.

"Yes..." he started sleepily and then remembered. "Yes, visits... where was I?"

"Graham, fancy not remembering where you were last night! I know."

He felt his heart thudding irregularly in his chest and a great tight ball rose into his throat, choking off the air. He sat up in bed and looked at her as straight as he could. She had looked away and was searching for somewhere to sit.

"I certainly do." She sounded serious and condemning. He couldn't speak; it would come out like a strangled cat and she would guess something was wrong. He cleared his throat and took a sip of the tea.

"You were visiting a young lady. Shame on you, McCreadie."

How on earth did she know? And did she therefore know everything? Or was she just guessing?

The tight ball of tension in his throat had loosened its grip a little with the sip of tea. He managed to get a few words out. "Yes, I need to visit young ladies as well as the old ones." It sounded neutral enough while he worked out how much she knew.

"And you were trying to get her to speak with her husband and get him to change his mind."

The relief that surged through Graham's body made him sink back into the pillows and even managed a smile.

"Yes, I went to see your pal Grace. I didn't go just to get him to change his mind. I was bothered about Grace and how she must have felt. Keith can be so angry and judgmental. I know she worries about that."

"Shame on you working behind his back like that. You know how to get round people. Anyway, she phoned me after you'd been to see her to say that Keith had agreed to come back onto the deacons' court as long as no one knew he'd resigned. She asked me to let you know."

"Oh, that's great." He was annoyed that his halfhearted efforts at persuading Keith back had actually been successful.

With that, Anne got up and left. Graham lay back down in the bed and remembered the night before, Sarah's face and her heavenly body... It was like a wonderful, invigorating dream – but it was real! He could still smell her, still hear her groans of delight.

He forced himself to get up: on Saturdays he made final preparations for the next day's service and he was more than usually behind with things. He made himself some toast and coffee and took them into his study to start work.

As he prepared his sermon, Graham's attention drifted repeatedly towards Sarah. Their first meetings had been passionate and physical but they had hardly known one another; now they had a relationship. It was like she was under his skin and was with him, around him, in his heart and mind all the time. He stared past the computer screen and daydreamed about sleeping all night with her and having breakfast together; even living with her. What a joy it would be for them to live together!

He forced himself to focus on the sermon, which was about full commitment to God, with no compromise. He could be strong on this, especially when people heard in his voice and saw in his demeanor that he was a role model for them. *It is astonishing how quickly and easily the conscience is put to sleep*, he reflected. He would like to preach on that some time, but he would be preaching to himself! *People who tell you that you need to go by your conscience don't know the half of it! Your conscience justifies what you do much more than it stops you misbehaving.* He had met convicts who could justify why they had killed a girlfriend or stabbed a

complete stranger. Now he found himself doing the same thing –
justifying his affair by telling himself that his marriage had
become loveless as well as sexless and telling himself that Sarah
had seduced him and she was far too stunning to resist. *The spirit
is willing, but my flesh is weak.* No, that was a sermon that would
have to wait.

He returned to the actual sermon: full commitment. A phrase
came to him – he must have read it somewhere, but it would do:
If Jesus isn't Lord of all, He isn't Lord at all. Then he would follow
this up with: *Now, what is it that* **you** *haven't surrendered to Jesus?*
Guilt was great: people actually loved being prodded into feeling
a little bit guilty; it comforted them to believe that their
consciences were still at work. But too much guilt was bad:
people became embarrassed and depressed if you reminded them
that they were actually much worse than they believed.

For a last-minute effort, this wasn't bad. Another one-liner
came to mind: *If being a Christian was a criminal offence, would there
be enough evidence to convict you?* He'd used it not so long ago in a
women's meeting, but that didn't matter. Most of them would
have forgotten anyway. Then his imagination played a little trick
on him as the phrase morphed: *If being an adulterer was a criminal
offence, would there be enough evidence to convict you?* Well, no, there
probably wouldn't be. Only Sarah knew and she wouldn't talk
about it. They would be very, very discrete and the unlikeliness
of their liaison was itself protection: even if someone suspected it,
no one would believe it.

A final one-liner sprang into his mind: *Which of us, if even the
least of our sins were written on our foreheads, would dare to leave the
house in the morning?* What a cracker! They would love that.

They did: people showed their adoration the next day as they
left, some patting his hand warmly as he shook theirs. It had gone
down like a dream. If he had taken time to think about the
hypocrisy of his position – preaching about commitment and
faithfulness while committing adultery – he would have not

dared to show his face to the public, never mind stand in front of 200 of them and preach. But he didn't think about it, perhaps because he knew what would come of such a thought.

The affair went on for something over a year. A few weeks after its start, Michael (who had developed something of an infatuation for Sarah and had not quite been stalking her, but it wasn't much short of that) stumbled upon the fact that Pastor Graham had been visiting her in the late evening and made the obvious deduction. When he spoke about it, none of the three people listening to his story came to the same conclusion, however. One concluded that Michael's own feelings for Sarah were clouding his judgment. The second told him that Pastor Graham would under no circumstances do something so wrong. The third (his father) completely believed him and even urged him to spill the beans. But then he added: *Mind you, they'll either hate you or ridicule you in every church in town!* Michael did nothing. A week or two later a little-believed story about Pastor Graham seeing Sarah went around town; it was said in the Baptist church that this was the devil trying to undermine his wonderful ministry. But neither Graham nor Sarah heard the rumor – and of course Anne would have been the last to hear.

The months went by and Michael started to doubt his own observations – he had seen his car; she had been up at the window in her nightie; she had blushed when a few days later he had mentioned Graham's name… Finally he decided that he had indeed been mistaken.

Brian Cannon, Catherine's neighbor, found out the truth. A security camera protecting the flat he owned next door to Sarah's had a motion sensor and captured each of Graham's frequent comings and goings. A devastating stroke, possibly brought on by the stress of finding out such a scandal, stopped him speaking about it. His wife had to be taken into care because Brian was both physically and verbally disabled.

Sarah was filled with guilt; she blamed herself for causing

Brian's stroke. She refused to see Graham for several weeks. When she met him again, in a garden center café some miles away, she announced that she was moving elsewhere. It would be better for them both in the long run, she explained. Indeed it was.

During the twelve months that the affair lasted, part of him hoped that he would be found out. For one thing, he wasn't a natural or accomplished liar. For another, he sensed that a judgment was coming on his behavior and he half thought that it may as well come quickly. He would leave the ministry and be with Sarah. But most of all, he wanted people to know that this beautiful and remarkable young woman had chosen him ahead of all the younger men in town. It was a silly thought and not one that he was proud of, but it was there.

In the first days after Sarah left, Graham sank into a kind of depression. For the first time in his career he asked to be relieved of preaching duties for three weeks. He told them he was deep in study of Paul's letter to the Ephesians and needed a break to listen to God. In leaving, Sarah had deprived him not only of someone whom he loved, but more significantly Graham had lost an admirer of the first order. What he had been seduced by was not simply Sarah's beauty, but also her admiration: it was like winning a first prize in front of everyone who mattered to him.

So when she left it was like he was suddenly devalued; he had been stripped of his prize. Their relationship had not become so strong that separation was painful for either of them but his life was flat and sad now that those wonderful eyes were no longer on him.

Immediately he tried to lose himself in Paul's letter to the Ephesians. He wanted to believe that it had something crucial to say to him at that critical moment of his life. When he read the fourth chapter, he found it:

You were taught, with regard to your former way of life, to put off your old self, which is being corrupted by its deceitful

desires; to be made new in the attitude of your minds; and to put on the new self, created to be like God in true right-eousness and holiness. Therefore each of you must put off falsehood and speak truthfully...
Ephesians 4:24–27

In one of those moments of clarity and insight, he saw that his own desire for Sarah had indeed been corrupting him. She had been like a drug and his addiction had nearly ruined him. He told himself that she hadn't even been so very interesting. The sex had been good, but that – oddly enough – had not mattered all that much to him. He suddenly saw that her rapid and painless departure meant one thing for sure: she had never really thought so highly of him after all. He had been her unattainable knight in shining amour and foolishly he had allowed himself to be captured. She would never have come away with him if their affair had been revealed.

He threw himself back into work. The need for popularity drove him to redouble his pastoral visits; the anger he felt at his loss added passion to his preaching. Twelve people attended the first church membership class; eight more came to the second and eventually 23 people joined the church. It was the biggest intake of new members for over thirty years. Sixteen of them were baptized in four services. Word was out: Graham McCreadie was on fire for God.

Occasionally Graham thought to himself: "If only they knew..." They never did; nor did anyone else. Years later he heard that Sarah had got married and had a daughter.

The problem with drugs is the pleasure they bring; or the pain they help us avoid. Graham was addicted to success and popularity more than ever. His ego had been battered by Catherine's sudden leaving; his newfound success in the church was ample compensation. Anne was more coruscating and cynical than ever; she knew an overinflated balloon when she saw one! But with each success came another challenge; every successive plaudit required more effort to win. Once your standards of success are raised, people start expecting success as a right. He knew that he had to find at least twenty people to baptize within a year, or he would feel a failure. He took to counting the numbers of people at church each week and checking on the total in the offering plate. He was deflated when the numbers went down – as they periodically did – and stupidly happy when they went back up. It was a ridiculous merry-go-round, which Anne could see with her usual harsh clarity but to which Graham was entirely blind.

One morning there was a letter from Brother Simon, written in improbably beautiful italic script, inviting him to tea at the Dominican retreat center. Now and then Simon invited past Enneagram students to meet together for support and encouragement. Graham usually found these meetings pleasant on the surface but underneath they niggled him: he knew full well that he wasn't "moving on" as they described it towards maturity. But he had committed himself long ago to going along, as indeed had the others in the group.

When he arrived he was surprised to find no other cars in the driveway. Brother Simon's bike stood leaning up against a wall in a cloister, otherwise there was no sign of anyone else. The center was closed to the public. He parked his shiny silver-grey car and walked to the side door. It opened before he reached it.

"Brother Simon, no less!" Graham greeted him warmly and hugged him. "Am I the first to arrive? It's not like me..."

"You're the only one to arrive. You're the only one I've invited."

Immediately Graham felt threatened. Simon would be able to question and probe in his deep and insightful way and Graham felt very vulnerable. What if he knew about Sarah? Simon had a way of knowing that often amazed people.

They chatted over tea and scones, which the hard-faced young housekeeper brought to them. Simon seemed to be blissfully unconcerned about dwindling numbers attending events at the Centre, nor about the reduction in numbers attending Mass in the Centre's ancient chapel. "We live in deeply unfavorable times, Graham. You must know that. The world today is obsessed with image and style; everyone sees himself as a star in his very own chat show. It's all about ego and bravado. There's no room for a spiritual life there – well, maybe I should say that the ego is the enemy of the Spirit and the ego is winning at the moment!"

Graham was silent. On some Sundays as he preached he thought about televising the services. He had fantasized about being broadcast live in the way some mega-churches in the US are. He wondered what it would be like to have TV cameras doing close-ups of his face, then panning round to catch the attentive and appreciative looks on the faces in the congregation. Now, as he took in Simon's words, he felt embarrassed.

"But you are not experiencing this with your people, are you? I understand you have problems with car parking: the neighbors are complaining. Lucky you. Is it true you're thinking of employing another minister?"

"Yes, the deacons want that. Not my idea, but they think it would reduce the pressure on me."

"And would it?"

When Simon asked a question like that Graham knew that there was a deeper and more demanding meaning behind it.

"No, it wouldn't."

"Because… ?" Simon invited him to explain.

"Because the expectations would go up a notch."

"And you are still playing the success game, are you?"

"It's better than the failure game," Graham blurted out, unthinkingly.

"Oh no it's not! In many ways Jesus' life was a succession of failures – people who rejected him, the rich young ruler who went away sadly, disciples who didn't understand the first thing about his ministry, being tried in a kangaroo court and killed in the most demeaning way. Not much success there. That's why his disciples all ran away at the end – they saw their master fail..."

Graham was defeated but exhilarated to be able to talk about it. "It's like being on a hamster wheel. I think I may drop with exhaustion one day."

"But you know what to do about it..."

"Yes. But... the spirit is willing..."

"At your age, after all your experience and training, and with such a successful church around you, and your flesh is still so very weak?" Simon could say such wounding things with grace and love!

"I'm still afraid that if I let go of my success thing, there'll be nothing there. Like an onion: take away all the layers and there's nothing left."

"God made you more than an onion! You need to stop staring into the mirror, Graham. Even though you like what you see there, you'll not find God there."

"Hmph! And where will I find Him, then? I see the changes in people's lives and I see God's work through me. I see the church growing and I know in my heart of hearts that it's the Spirit's work, not mine." Graham was defending himself as best he could.

"You'll find Him like Joshua did – not in the noisy thunderstorm of success, but in the quiet emptiness of your heart."

Simon got up, took hold of a pile of vestments and put them on, readying himself for Mass. His mind seemed to be elsewhere, as if Graham was not there. He left the room and Graham found himself alone. He got up and wandered towards the fire crackling in the large hearth. A wide and ornately-decorated mirror stretched across the breadth of the broad chimney. He looked at himself for a long time. Then, gazing straight into his own eyes, he laughed, long and loud. Then he looked away.

Spiritual Exercises for 3s

1   Why do you think Graham's growth started when he could laugh at himself?

2   *"You are my Son, whom I love; with you I am well pleased."* In what ways do you perform in order to win God's approval and others' plaudits?

3   *To you, LORD, I call; you are my Rock* (**Psalm 28:1**). David's awareness was of God as the solid ground of his being. Reflect and meditate on this until you truly sense its truth for you.

4   "I'm really not that interested in myself," Graham told his wife. The truth was, he didn't like to remove his mask or admit his weaknesses. Think about your own weaknesses and talk about it honestly with a friend.

5   Pray about this weakness, using these words as a guide: *But [God] said to me, "My grace is sufficient for you, for my power is made perfect in weakness." Therefore I will boast all the more gladly about my weaknesses, so that Christ's power may rest on me."*

6   One of the core questions which Christian faith puts to us is this: *What good will it be for someone to gain the whole world, yet forfeit their soul?* (**Matthew 16:26**) In quiet reflection, think about the ways you have starved your soul in pursuit of "gaining the whole world."

7   Read David's story in **1 Samuel 16**. David went on to commit adultery and kill to hide the fact. So why did God choose him? What did he see in David's heart? What does he see in yours?

Harry's Story: Type 9

Peace I leave with you; my peace I give you. I do not give to you as the world gives. Do not let your hearts be troubled and do not be afraid.
John 14:27

And the peace of God, which transcends all understanding, will guard your hearts and your minds in Christ Jesus.
Philippians 4:7

Harry was born one bright, breezy sunny Saturday afternoon in July, so as not to be a nuisance to anyone – or so he would tell others, laughing. It was ideal: his older brother Joshua and sister Nadine were sent to the neighbors because their children were keen for the company in the school holidays. Harry's father was able to be at the birth without taking a precious day off work and the following day, the Sunday, grandparents, two aunts and five friends came in a tidy procession of visits to see the latest addition to the Jennings family. When he cried in those first days of life, his mother listened as if entranced: it sounded more like a gentle alarm than a cry for food or in pain, a gentle reminder rather than a demand for attention. When he woke hungry during the night the sounds he made were almost apologetic: *Sorry about waking you, Mum, but could I get fed, please?*

And he grew up like that – quiet, not wanting to be a fuss, everybody's friend. He had a quality of peace about him which hung around him like an aura and he had a capacity to be a buffer between warring parties – even his older siblings – which became legendary in the family. More than once his mother, looking for him to do something he was meant to be doing, entered the room where he was sitting and failed to notice him there. By the time he looked up to see who had come into the room, she had gone.

He hadn't heard her calls, nor even noticed the door opening.

In truth he lived in a kind of bubble, a parallel world really, where everything was calm and easy. On planet H.J. there were no demands on him and there was no conflict at all because nothing very much happened. Harry was well aware that he had his own personal world, because it was a great deal more real than the one his contemporaries seemed to inhabit. He often resented the way that other people dragged him out of his contentment into their hassles, problems and demands – especially demands.

Harry wasn't a lazy boy (although that was an accusation thrown carelessly at him by several exasperated teachers awaiting his completed homework, for instance); rather it was that he didn't notice that things needed to be done: his clothes put in the dirty washing basket, his cup back in the kitchen, the milk brought in from the doorstep. He would do his homework so long as he remembered, or latterly was reminded that it needed to be done. Somehow the list "Stuff which people want me to do" was much less interesting and fun than the list "Stuff which I like doing."

He was a renowned under-performer. He eventually learned how to talk, around the age of three, and his words were so pronounced in such a cute and childish way that no one had the hardness of heart necessary to correct him. The way he spoke the word 'sugar' would melt the heart of the toughest onlooker: "thoo-gah". Around the time Harry was preparing to go to secondary school he decided that his childish lisping needed to go, so it went, almost overnight, as if it were a skin he had decided to cast off. Reading seemed to be particularly pointless: after all, he could watch the TV or have someone else read him a story if necessary. So he ambled slowly through the learning-to-read books until eventually one of the 'special' children had overtaken him. He became aware that one or two of his friends thought him to be a bit slow, so he made an effort for a couple of weeks and leapt three books ahead.

What he excelled at was in sport. He played anything he was invited to, from football to hockey and water polo, but he loved cricket most of all: it had a rhythm that worked wonders for him and he delighted in batting. He would step up to the crease every time firmly persuaded that he was doing so to score the winning runs for England in the Cricket World Cup final. Friends always wanted him on their side, not just because he was good but because he was such a great guy to have on your team: a kind, fun-loving person who had not one ounce of malice in him and who always believed his side could and would win.

Mr. and Mrs. Jennings grew used to the parents' nights and the recital of the familiar comments about under-performance, but it was very hard to tell their third child that he needed to be a bit more ruthless, organized and determined. That would have been like wanting a chocolate cake to be spicy or a pancake to be well-risen: it just went against his very nature and they knew it very well. An organized Harry would have been weird! There were times when Mrs. Jennings would have liked to point out to the teachers that even though he might be academically weak, he was sometimes a wonder at home, keeping proud Joshua and sometimes-annoying Nadine apart, often physically. This kind of skill was not valued, still less taught at school, of course.

He left school, therefore, with a motley collection of exam results which would have probably got him a place at an inferior college of higher education of some sort, had he wanted to pursue his education further, but he didn't. The truth was, he wanted to play cricket semi-professionally but he had narrowly failed to get into the county junior cricket academy. His second option was football and although there were far more possibilities and openings for that sport, he was politely refused by three clubs. Two of them quietly told his mother that they thought he was quite good, but they thought he was unlikely to withstand the rough-and-tumble of the world of professional soccer. They were wrong; he would have let the stress bounce off his back just as he did everything else. Whether he would have remembered to turn up each day for the training sessions was another matter: probably not.

Jennifer, his long-term girlfriend (they met when she moved in next door and they were both 13) moved to university in London. They told each other that they would see each other during the holidays and that he would visit her on weekends, but somehow it didn't work out that way and by Christmas she had broken off their relationship. By then even Harry had realized that it wasn't working out and he didn't mind very much when he saw her walking hand-in-hand with the young man she had met at university who was apparently from a rich family in the North East. He smiled benignly at both of them, while Jennifer blinked in her delightfully embarrassed way and the new man looked on bemused.

By then he had found work with the insurance company, in the customer services section. He had applied to them as an apprentice clerk but when he did their aptitude assessments they had noticed that he dealt with people much better than with letters and bills and even severe stress didn't seem to get to him. Keith, his immediate boss, called him "Teflon Man" because he seemed to have an almost untouchable quality about him – he never seemed to be to blame for mistakes even though he sometimes ignored procedures and guidelines. He seemed to have a knack of tiptoeing untouched through problems, arguments and conflicts while dirt was flying from all sides, but none stuck on him. And everyone liked him!

"How can there be peace," Jehu replied, "as long as all the idolatry and witchcraft of your mother Jezebel abound?"
2 Kings 9:22

When Nadine, Harry's sister, went off with Sandy, though, things got tough around the office. Keith, who was on the same grade as her in a different department, was furious: he had made his opinion clear on several occasions when he had overheard her talking about her "secret" rendezvouses with the wealthy businessman whom everyone (Keith included) knew to be Sandy. Sandy was married to the daughter of Keith's pastor. Although he didn't approve of Catherine (she was flirty and edgy, even with Keith himself) he was angry that the sickness of marital breakdown had struck so near the heart of his church. At least this was the way that Keith explained it in his owl-eyed and tight-mouthed way one lunchtime when he had Harry on his own in the canteen. Harry nodded as he usually did and muttered something about it all being very sad for everyone involved, them being so young and so on. Keith's reply was: "*It's not just sad, Harry; it's wrong.*"

Harry didn't see it that way. He was very young in the ways of relationships and he had the idea that sometimes people made mistakes when they got married so that A who was meant for B somehow got hitched with C, so that B went off with D. Little surprise that a while later they should reorganize themselves so that A was now with B and C with D. There was a beautiful and naïve simplicity in the way Harry thought about these things, so the idea that it was 'wrong' didn't really enter into his thinking. Besides, what business was it of Keith's? Why would someone want to kick up a fuss about it? To Harry, it was like a fisherman trying to brew up a storm: who in their right minds would do that? Why would you want to make life difficult for yourself?

His sister Nadine had dated Sandy for a few months when they were both at school. They had a petty argument over something and Harry gathered from the gloom in the living room one day that Nadine had 'dumped' Sandy. At the time he didn't have a clue what that meant. His brother Joshua got his tuppenceworth in:

"Word on the street, Naddie, is that you dumped Sandy

because Austin Knowles-Hart has become available."

Harry hated it when his brother and sister argued with each other, but since he was starting to get interested in this dating thing he tried to follow what they were saying as he pretended to watch the football on the TV.

"You are despicable Joshua Jennings! That is a total lie. I don't even know Austin."

"Oh, Nadine that is a big black nasty fib!" Joshua was getting worked up. Harry could tell from the way his voice had gone quiet. "You danced with him at the school ball and Mary Fellowes saw him kissing you in the library – or was it you snogging him?"

Nadine leapt from her seat and attacked her brother, who easily fended her off by holding her arms off. "Tell me that isn't true!" he concluded, struggling with her. She turned away and stomped off up the stairs.

It turned out to be true, but the last person AK-H was likely to date was Nadine. He was far more ambitious and had set his sights on the daughter of a very rich Earl Something-or-other. By the time that Nadine finally realized all this, Sandy was seeing Catherine and it was quite serious between them. According to Joshua though, Catherine was dating atheist Sandy only because it upset her mother and she seemingly thought it was "cool". It wouldn't last in his opinion. Within a couple of months they were engaged and then they got married.

Now Sandy had realized his mistake and was back with Nadine. Harry didn't see anything much wrong with that.

"You see, Harry, it's not just sad, it's wrong," Keith went on, reddening a little. The reason why it's wrong is that it's really bad for relationships if you think that you can just walk away when things get tough."

Harry wanted to tell Keith that he thought that his sister had always loved Sandy, even through his marriage to Catherine. He knew that she had found it hard to date anyone seriously as a result, because she had told him so in a drunken rant one Sunday evening a year or so ago. He could also have told Keith that he knew Nadine and Sandy had been seeing each other for some time because he would drop her off at the house after they had been out. But Harry said nothing; he hoped Keith would stop.

"I know she's your sister, so you've got to be on her side. I'm sorry if I've gone on about it, Harry." Keith now looked apologetic. "I just feel strongly about these things."

Harry smiled and nodded. He felt like one of those big buffers sailors use to protect the ship when it docks. He gathered from Keith's expression that he had stopped now. Harry thought he looked very unhappy, but he had the impression that Christians were often unhappy: if they weren't guilty, they were angry; if they weren't angry, they were shocked.

"I'd er… really like to take you along to one of our services some time, Harry…" Coming from Keith the words sounded like a threat, or a punishment, but Harry could sense that some sort of response was necessary. He managed a vague and indefinite "Hm…" which Keith nodded at, as if it had been a wholehearted "Oh, I'd love that!"

Woe to you when everyone speaks well of you, for that is how their ancestors treated the false prophets.
Luke 6:25–27

Oddly enough, it was that afternoon that he met Ellen – or, as Nadine would say, it was then that Ellen met Harry. She had been chosen from some 200 applicants for the post of Customer Services Manager so she came highly commended. She winked at him when she came into the room with her boss, as if she knew him already. She approached him a few minutes later while he sorted through a pile of customer satisfaction forms.

"My name's Ellen. I'm starting work here on Monday. I'll be your boss, but don't worry, I'm very nice!"

Harry took an instant dislike to her. She seemed to be fake and pushy. He smiled at her broadly and said, "Yes, I'm sure you're very nice. I heard also that you were very good. Do you live in town?"

"No, I live in Birmingham, but my house is up for sale. Five people coming to see it this weekend. Maybe I'm selling it too cheap. Still, it's good to get the interest. I'm going to buy here. I mean, we get good deals on mortgages, don't we?"

"I think so," Harry answered. "I live with my parents, so I don't –"

"–need a mortgage?" She was finishing his sentences for him. She was going to be a handful to work with, Harry thought.

"I'm sorry, I promised to have these ready half an hour ago… it's the end of the month, so they need these for the reports…"

Ellen touched his hand as she turned away. "No problem. See you Monday." She winked again; she liked the look of him. He smiled broadly; he disliked that wink already.

He didn't see much of her when she started work, as she was given an induction course. She dropped by on Tuesday afternoon along with a male colleague who had also just started with the business. It looked to Harry as if they were close friends, because Ellen leaned up against him as they stood looking at the wall-charts outlining customer satisfaction. Finally late on Thursday afternoon he saw her settling into her glassed-off office and he assumed she had started work. She sat at her desk making phone calls and didn't come out once. Perhaps something unfortunate had happened, thought Harry. When he left he looked towards her to wave goodbye, but she was deep in conversation on the phone and didn't notice him.

She was already at work when he arrived the next day. Her door was slightly ajar. He peered in, smiling. "Been here all night?" he joked.

"No. I like to start work early. I like to be on top of things. Can we meet to discuss roles and responsibilities at 3:30 this afternoon?" She sounded very official and here wasn't a trace of a smile, let alone a wink.

"Yes, no problem," he replied. He was supposed to finish work at 3 pm on Fridays, as he started half an hour early each day, but he didn't want to be awkward during her first week as his boss.

She was on the phone when he arrived for the meeting, a minute or two early, and kept him waiting five minutes while she ended the call. As she was asking him to get them both a cup of coffee, her phone rang again and she embarked on a call which was still going on when he returned with their coffees. Her door was shut and when he went to open it she signaled through the glass for him to wait. He sipped his coffee while she finished her call and kept a little in the bottom of the cup so that it wouldn't look rude. She opened the door in a rush, taking him by the hand into her office as if he were a child in a supermarket queue.

"I'm so sorry to keep you waiting," she gushed. "First week at work and everyone's wanting a bit of me. It'll be fine this time next week. Shall we have our meeting then? Same time, next week? It's a bit late now, don't you think? I wanted to get away by four. Look, it's ten past. Is that OK? Hey, thanks for the coffee. It'll probably be cold now. Never mind."

It seemed to Harry that her sentences were like threads that she drew from an immense piece of material; few of them ever got tied up and completed.

"No problem. See you Monday. Next Friday's fine. Have a good weekend!" She was looking away now, and talking into her handbag, as if there was someone else waiting for her there. He left.

She was only five minutes late for their meeting the next Friday. He handed her the coffee and she placed it without comment on a high shelf as if it was a specimen that she was keeping out of interest.

"I'm a results-orientated manager, Harry," she began. "I have targets to reach and if we reach them, I'll be happy. If we don't, I'll blame you."

Harry smiled broadly. She was looking away, but when she looked back he realized she was serious. "You do your job properly, I'll leave you alone. I'm into empowerment. I'm not going to micro-manage you and set unrealistic outcomes when all that's needed is proper attention to the necessary drivers and measures. We know the score, don't we? It's not rocket science, after all. So, let's just touch base once a month, last Friday of the month, this time and we'll be the best of friends."

He was dismissed then, but she called him back.

"Hey, Harry, d'you drive? Can you drive a van? I lost my license." He nodded agreeably.

"Are you really really busy Sunday? I need someone to drive the van for me. You wouldn't like to be a sweetheart, would you? Could you?" She was holding his arm and looking into his eyes. As he looked, he thought for a moment that she looked like an upright pig, her bright eyeliner accentuating her slightly bulbous eyes. He knew that she would be annoyed if he told her that he was playing cricket and it was the semi-final so he didn't want to miss it. He was going to bat at three, and it was his big chance to impress the Captain.

"I can... sure... just text me the time and place," he said and was relieved when she removed her hand from his arm and winked at him as she turned away. Sure, got it here – the number. You're a real sweetheart and I love you so much for this. I won't forget it. Brilliant. See you then!" and with that she was looking into her handbag again, talking to herself, he thought. He wondered what he should say to the captain, calling off less than two days beforehand. He would need to say he had an injury of some kind.

He got the text that evening, asking him to arrive at an address on the far side of Birmingham at 9 o'clock Sunday morning. He was annoyed to have to miss the semi-final game, but he thought that he could say "No" to the cricket skipper more easily than to Ellen.

So he set the alarm for 7:30 on Sunday morning and arrived five minutes late at Ellen's small house on the west side of Birmingham. At the front was a set of double doors, so when he pressed on the bell he couldn't hear if it rang inside. He waited a few moments and then rang again. There was no response. He went to the side of the house to see if there was another door, and came to a fence with a small gate leading to the back door, but there was an angry-looking Bull Terrier standing guard and he decided against risking it. He went to the front again and this time banged on the door hard. He waited two minutes and tried again. There was no response. He began to wonder if he had arrived at the wrong house, so he checked the text he had received and saw that he was where he had been asked to come. He realized that he had her mobile number as she had texted him, so he decided to ring her. After five rings a sleepy-sounding voice replied.

"Yes? It's very early. What is it?"

"Hi, it's Harry here. You asked me to come at 9. I've been ringing your bell and banging on the door for a quarter of an hour."

"I'll be right down."

Ellen appeared at the door a minute later, her hair bedraggled and smears of makeup around her eyes. She turned back into the house without speaking and wandered sleepily into what Harry took to be the kitchen.

"Coffee or tea?" she shouted over the sound of the tap running into the kettle.

"Tea for me, please, Ellen. Thanks. Two sugars and milk." He sat down awkwardly on the sofa and looked around. For someone who was moving house, everything looked very organized and tidy. Or maybe she hadn't started putting things in boxes yet, he thought to himself.

"You seem very calm… considering you're moving," he shouted back. There was no reply.

Ellen arrived with two cups of coffee. "Sorry, no milk. You don't take sugar do you?" She passed him a mug.

"It doesn't matter," he replied, trying not to sound too gloomy.

"The girls from work took me out last night. Got totally plastered. Which was a nuisance – I've not packed anything yet. Oh, the van needs to be picked up before 10. What time did you say it was?"

"It's twenty past nine."

"Oh, well you'd better go get it. It's probably twenty minutes' drive. I meant to phone you to tell you to collect it on the way, 'cos you passed it on the way here. Never mind, you'll be able to drop it off on your way back."

Harry felt himself tensing inside with annoyance as he smiled benignly at Ellen. She reached into her purse and handed him two ten pound notes. It's Macro Van rental, near the Parkhouse roundabout, just down the Leehampton road a bit. Guy called Bob should be there. I'll get ready while you get it; should be all set for when you get back – you'll probably be best part of an hour."

Harry placed his mug of coffee on the table, got up and went out. He felt his feet plodding in the way they sometimes did when he was frustrated. For a short moment he imagined himself walking out to the middle of the cricket ground, his bat tucked under his arm, fastening his gloves as he walked confidently to the crease. He started up his car and drove off. He was hitting the first ball confidently through the covers for four, to shouts of approval and applause from the rest of the team. He negotiated the first roundabout, but when he came to the second one leading onto the 'A' road he saw that it was closed for resurfacing work and he was diverted onto a small country lane. As it wound left and right, he was striking the ball with ever-greater confidence and now he was facing Wes Scott, the other side's wickedly fast bowler who scared most batsmen to bits. The first ball was 'in the slot' and he swung it gracefully back over Wes' head for six. The second ball was an angry bouncer directed at his head; Harry stepped neatly over to off and clattered the ball backward of square for six. He didn't notice the yellow diversion sign pointing to his left and he drove straight on, this time picturing Wes' angry face as he walked back to his mark. It was a generous half-volley on leg, which Harry clipped effortlessly over midwicket for the third six of the over. Cheers from the skipper and admiring glances from Emily, his girlfriend, whom Harry liked very much and whom he had lusted after for two years or more. He had just pictured her face when he had to step on his brakes to avoid hitting a tractor.

When he finally managed to pass the tractor, he realized he was lost. He drove another ten miles until he came to a main road signposted to Wrexham. He had no idea where he was and there was no one to ask.

Two hours later he arrived back at Ellen's with a van.

"Harry, what the hell have you been up to? I've been worried sick. I thought you had had an accident. I tried ringing you, but you didn't answer the phone."

"No, I left it in the car. I got lost 'cos of a diversion. When I finally got to Macro vans it was eleven o'clock and he had gone. I had to go to Birmingham to get a van." He didn't tell her that he had had to pay a £140 for it.

"Oh well, you're here now. Now, can you help me pack some stuff? Why don't you do here and I'll do upstairs?"

It was nearly eleven in the evening by the time he carried the last box into her new flat on the third floor.

"When'll you take the van back?" Ellen asked, only half interested.

"Tomorrow. Will they say anything if get to work late? Maybe 10-ish?"

"You can't do that; it's the first Monday of the month. Options meeting. You need to report back. It'll need to be after work. They won't close till six, or seven, I'd imagine."

He took the van back the following evening after work and was charged a further £120. He thought about mentioning it to Ellen in the hope that she might pay some of it, but decided against it. It had been his mistake, after all. He couldn't expect her to pay for that, he decided.

When she invited him to her flat three weeks later, he was too taken aback to find an excuse to refuse. He had no idea she wanted to be friends with him. He disliked the sight of her and was getting thoroughly annoyed with her whining tone when she was worked up about something. He told himself that he would go to the party, but talk to someone else if possible, so that she would realize that he wasn't interested in being friends with her. He imagined himself chatting to a pretty girl who looked like Emily.

He turned up at the party on the Friday evening and Ellen immediately took off his jacket and wrapped herself around him. She steered him into the living room, where a gaggle of loud and ugly people stared as she held him close to her side. "This is my lovely friend Harry. No girls, you can't. He's mine." She took hold of his hand and didn't let go. When he moved towards the door, she clasped him more firmly and pulled him back. She wrapped her other arm around his neck and kissed him firmly on the lips and the other guests watched. He got the impression she was doing it to impress them, but he found himself unable to resist without looking either very rude or clumsy.

The evening passed slowly. She let him go when she went to the toilet, but was back before he could start up a conversation with a woman whom he recognized from Accounts. Ellen took hold of his arm and pulled him away. He could feel himself getting angry, but he told himself that she was his boss, after all, and if he made a fuss she could make life very difficult at work.

The door closed behind them and he realized he was in her bedroom. She locked the door with a key which she placed down the front of her dress.

Harry didn't speak about that evening to anyone. The next morning he told his parents that he had stayed with a friend the night before as he had drunk too much alcohol to be safe driving the car.

So he stumbled into a loveless relationship with Ellen in which they usually drank a lot and then slept together. She seemed to have nothing to talk about and was not interested in him. She liked to take him with her when she was visiting friends. After three weeks and their fifth encounter, he decided to tell her that he didn't want to meet her again. He sat in his room at home for a whole evening working out how to tell her without making her angry.

The next evening he collected her from her flat in his car. She wasn't ready when he arrived, so he had to wait for her. She eventually ran into the room and told him to come quickly. When they were sitting in the car, he announced:

"Ellen, I've been thinking about us. I've really decided that I want to stay friends with you, but not for us to date."

"What? Why? Is there something the matter with me?" she asked.

"No, of course not. It's not that, it's just that... I really..."

"Look, Harry, we're late. Can we talk about this as we go? I said we'd be there at eight and now you've made us half an hour late already. Rachel and Gwen will think we've done a bunk."

He started up the car and drove towards the town center.

"Is there someone else? Do you want to see someone else? I wouldn't mind if you did – as long as it didn't clash."

"No, of course there's no one else. But I don't want to date anyone regularly just now. I'm not ready for that."

"OK. I don't mind. It doesn't need to be regular. Just now and then, OK?" She was getting irritated and he didn't want her to be in that mood when they met up with Rachel and Gwen.

Harry nodded and decided to drop the issue, sensing that he had won half his point. He hadn't; she went on phoning him twice a week as she had done and wouldn't take "No" for an answer. But he knew that it would take him weeks, if not months, to work up the courage to try again to break it off.

The TV was on; Harry was waiting for the cricket to start. In his mind's eye he was halfway through his maiden innings for Worcestershire, brought into the side when five of the squad were injured in a minibus crash. It was the Cup final and so the TV cameras were there – it was broadcast live in Britain and India. A good performance here might well set up a lucrative 6-week contract with the famous Indian Champions' Cup, to which star performers from around the world were invited and paid huge sums of money. He had come in with his county in a hopeless position, needing 108 runs from 6 overs and only two wickets left. No side had ever won from such an impossible situation, but he had smashed 44 runs from his first twelve balls and then... Browne was out LBW and the last man came out to bat. Harry would need to not only make the runs but also keep the strike, because young Catterick could no more bat than fly to the moon. And all this in his maiden innings!

He vaguely heard his mother shouting something. His attention drifted towards Ellen and a thought which he had had several times already: how could he be dating someone whom he didn't like? In fact, he found her selfish, irritating and domineering. She was overweight and physically definitely not his type. He didn't like her friends – they were so loud and boisterous, and usually got drunk. So why was he dating her?

The new bowler was Imran, who played for Pakistan. His first ball was a real loosener – wide, short and outside off – Harry swung gloriously, using that 'inside-out' stroke he had seen on TV and the ball sailed over cover for six. The crowd were on their feet, sensing drama on an epic scale... That was his fifty and there were just 50 runs needed now...

The truth was, she was his boss, so he couldn't easily say, "No." But she was taking advantage of him. It was abuse. Maybe he should report her to HR. He knew he couldn't do that; what evidence did he have, anyway? She would just say that he had freely agreed to go out with her. It would at least bring the relationship to an end, though. But at what cost? There would be a fuss and argument. People would find out. Life at work would become impossible. Getting a new job would not be easy – employers didn't like staff who annoyed the boss.

The next ball was a beauty, right in the slot on or outside off stump. He knew he had to play it. Just as he did so, the ball cut away and he edged it. In slow motion he watched it sail up and straight towards Jim Ellis, their captain, whose hands were like buckets. He saw the ball turn lazily on its axis and thump calami-tously into Ellis' grateful palms. Harry's heart fell; disap-pointment surged through him like a dead weight. Just as he turned away, ready to walk disconsolately back to the pavilion, the ball inexplicably turned in Ellis' hands and dropped as slowly as a feather towards the grass. Quick as lightning, Ellis stuck his foot out to kick the ball up before it landed. It sailed towards Harry as he stood, unbelieving, at the crease. It hit his left pad and landed harmlessly on the grass. Harry raised his right eyebrow towards Ellis as he stood there speechless with anger and then turned away to ready himself for the next ball.

He heard his mother's voice again, this time a little louder, but he had no idea what she was saying. She appeared in front of him. "Are you deaf, Harry? I said, That's Ellen on the phone for you."

"Oh, is it? Oh... no... well... can you tell her I'm out?"

"What? Don't you want to talk to her? She is your girlfriend. Of have you fallen out? I'm not going to lie to her."

With a huge effort Harry lifted himself from the sofa and went to the phone in the hallway, where his mother had left the handset on its side by the phone. Carefully he hung the handset back up on the cradle and then moved it slightly to one side so that it would be off the hook. It was a trick he was practiced in. He checked that he had indeed switched off his mobile in his pocket and then went back to watch the cricket.

While the presenters did their introductions and talked about the wicket, Harry decided to complete his Cup final innings. Where was he? Fifty runs left, wasn't it? Next ball drifting down leg, easily glanced off the thigh pad for four; couple more for a back foot drive, a six from a full toss and a quick single to keep the strike. Two overs left. First ball is a wide and Harry swings hard: it flies off an edge way over gulley for six. Then smash, crunch, drive – three sixes on the trot to bring them within 13 runs of the most improbable victory ever... in the history of the game anywhere in the world. Great ball next up – no runs scored. Last ball he has to run a single to keep the strike: a deft flick like the great Sachin Tendulkar brings him the run, while the fielders just gasp at his skill.

Talking of Tendulkar: the first and second balls are driven imperiously through the covers for four each. He holds the pose for the cameras. Four needed for the win, and for his hundred. They're all expecting the next ball to get walloped, but he spots the slower ball which swings in and he defends it, wisely. The bowler nods his approval. The fourth ball is well up to him but he steps back in his crease and with an effortless straight-batted push he drives it back past the bowler for four.

It's all over. The cheering is deafening, the crowd are on their feet – even the opposing fans! Harry walks back, his bat aloft all the way. He sees the Sky TV crew waiting to interview him but he turns away towards the pavilion, because she is there, waving and cheering too. The skipper isn't with her. She throws her arms around his neck and kisses him passionately on the lips. He tries to speak: "But what about – " she stops him with a finger on his mouth.

"I have always fancied you. I ditched him this morning. Come on, let's go. We can leave in my car…"

Ellen grew genuinely very fond of Harry: she was often amazed at his calmness and steadiness under pressure. She never heard him raise his voice or try to argue with a customer on the phone. She wished she had some of his skill in not rising to the bait. She told herself on several occasions that he must really be in love with her, or he wouldn't put up with her. His patience with her when she moved house was amazing; on a date, often she would keep him waiting for half an hour or more and he never complained. He was so sweet!

On the other hand she knew how difficult she was; not for nothing had she been known as "The Bitch" at her previous job. She had a big ego and she wasn't frightened of showing it – or so she reasoned. "That's the way I am – like it or lump it!" she would say to her girlfriends sometimes when they complained.

One Friday evening her friend Glenda phoned as she was getting ready to go out. She knew that Glenda had her eyes on Harry and Ellen enjoyed rubbing her nose in it. "He's so totally hot in bed, Glenda, I don't let him stay during the week 'cos I wouldn't be able to work the next day. We don't sleep for more than a couple of hours."

She heard Glenda take a deep breath. "It's you, Ellen, you beast! I've heard about your sexual prowess. It's a secret all over town." Ellen was oblivious to the irony. "Anyway, you push off and have a good time. See you next week."

The following Wednesday evening she had been working late and she picked up some fish and chips from the shop near Glenda's house. She was nearly an hour early, but she decided that she was so late she wouldn't go home first. She wandered in through the back door as she usually did and was surprised to find no one in the kitchen or the lounge. Usually her mother was around – perhaps, she told herself, she was at the bingo. She sat down on a kitchen chair and started eating her fish and chips. She could hear Glenda moving around upstairs in her bedroom. She had eaten half when she heard a groan. She thought it might be Glenda's mother; perhaps she was unwell upstairs.

She took a mouthful of fish and scampered out of the kitchen and up the stairs. The doors were all shut. Countless times she had been in Glenda's house and she knew her way with her eyes shut. She opened Glenda's bedroom door and heard the groaning somewhat louder. It was Glenda and the source of her pleasure was Harry, who for what seemed like two or three minutes was unaware that they had been disturbed. When he turned round he saw Ellen standing in the doorway with fish dripping from her lips.

"What the hell is going on here?"

With a composure that amazed even Harry, he said, "I should think you know very well what's going on. Why don't you shut the door on your way out? We've not finished yet."

The last of the fish dropped from Ellen's mouth. To Harry, whose internal laughter was fuelled by months of pent-up rage, it seemed that her eyes might follow the fish in dropping from her face. She turned slowly around and walked down the stairs with the tread of one bereaved as well as shocked. She sat, dumbly, on the sofa in the lounge.

An hour or so later Harry came downstairs almost whistling with contentment. He paused briefly when he saw Ellen, but said nothing as he went into the kitchen to make coffee for himself and Glenda.

Ellen stood trembling with rage in the doorway. "How could you, you dirty scheming, devious little rat?"

"Don't you think that's a really obvious thing to say?" Harry's heart didn't miss a beat. He was on top of the world. "I'm sure you could find something cleverer than that."

"Why?" She was crying now, tears flowing unchecked from her eyes.

"I got so sick of your selfishness, Ellen: the times you kept me waiting, the way you ignored me at parties, how you always took me for granted, the money you borrowed and didn't pay back, how you didn't ask me what I wanted to do but insisted on doing your thing."

"But… you…" she was gasping for breath between huge sobs. Harry almost felt sorry for her. Almost. "You never… said anything! You never complained."

"I don't complain," Harry responded. My mum told you that. "I do anything for a quiet life, eh?"

"But Glenda? You know she's my friend."

"I know she's not your friend. She's as sick of you as I am."

"Are you…" Ellen felt her body heave with the emotion of the question she felt compelled to ask. "Are you in love?"

"Hell no," Harry replied. "But Glenda is so hot in bed. We really do it for each other – big time!" He pushed past her with the mugs of coffee and walked nonchalantly upstairs.

Peace I leave with you; my peace I give you. I do not give to you as the world gives.
John 14:27

Years later Harry completed a degree course at King's College, Cambridge. Ellen, now Personnel Manager for the whole business, had negotiated day release at a local college for him so that he could study for university entry. She had long since given up hoping that they would date once again, but she knew she owed him for the months of abuse she had handed out to him. In moments of clarity and insight she had seen that.

Harry hugely enjoyed King's: the history and ceremony, the debate, the fabulous and ancient surroundings had made him feel very special. He had changed; he had grown. During his first year his tutor spotted him one evening walking slowly through the Quad towards the river Cam. "Harry, it's me, Geoffrey!"

"Oh, good evening. I was lost in thought…"

"About what, may I ask?" He had such a gentle and kind manner, Harry told him right out.

"I feel humbled by all this. I really don't deserve all this. My ex set it all up for me; it's crazy, but it's like someone else should have had this place, not me."

Geoffrey stopped by the bridge and looked at Harry.

"Young Jennings – you are still young by my standards! You have a right to be here. D'you know that prose poem by Max Ehrmann – *Desiderata*?" Harry shook his head. Geoffrey went on: "You are a child of the universe, no less than the trees and the stars; you have a right to be here." A deep truth resonated within Harry as he heard these words, as if he had heard them before. Geoffrey hadn't finished: "It's too easy playing the 'I'm so humble no one notices me' game, Harry. That's not what you're here for. You're bigger than that."

So each time he crossed the bridge – most days – he would say to himself, "I have a right to be here." Towards the end of second year he started to believe it.

As he walked ceremonially into the graduation hall with the Latin ceremony ringing in his ears he saw his parents and Joshua and Nadine sitting in a neat row, their faces revealing pride and astonishment in equal parts. But Harry was no longer astonished in himself; he believed now, he believed in himself and this ceremony was the proof of his self-belief.

He remained in Cambridge for a few days after graduation to tidy up his things and say his farewells to friends. He had no work lined up, but Ellen had sent him 'welcome back' messages from his old work urging him to return. He went and sat for a final time in the magnificent Chapel of King's College. Once or twice over the previous three years the splendor of the music and the occasion had made him wonder if there was anything more to it, but he had rejected faith as simple wishful thinking.

But now as he listened to the quivering beauty of Taverner's *Magnificat Collegium Regale*, the Eastern notes adding mystery to the reverence, a powerful awareness of the presence of God filled him and awed him. Simultaneously he recalled with genuine pride in himself how those hundreds of people had gazed at him in the graduation hall: it wasn't everyone who gained a First from Cambridge! He sensed himself in the midst of a mighty swirl of life, buzzing and shimmering and shouting, with love and hate rolling around with conflict and resolution and anger and calm. For perhaps the first time in his adult life he felt no desire to escape that bustling turmoil. Instead, he sensed he was being held in the very center of it all, in a beautiful stillness, by the hand of One whom he was just then beginning to know.

Spiritual Exercises for 9s

1   *"Harry was born one bright, breezy sunny Saturday afternoon in July, so as not to be a nuisance to anyone…"* Do you notice a tendency in yourself to avoid making your true needs known? Note down some examples.

2   *"On planet H.J. there were no demands…"* Do you 'check out' of reality like this? Does it happen because you feel threatened?

3   Where does God want you to be: here and now, or in your inner dreamland? Honestly, where is he most likely to meet you?

4   "Why would you want to make life difficult for yourself?" might be a kind of 'theme- question' for many 9s. Reflect on a time you avoided the difficult choice or failed to stand up for someone or something. What did you miss out on then? Was no one else affected, do you think?

5   Genuine humility and self-denial are possible only when you know and love yourself. What are the areas where you most often claim to be humble, but in fact you're just hiding away? Pray about them.

6   Riso and Hudson (*Wisdom of the Enneagram*, p. 330) point out that many 9s tend to rely on a mixture of "homey aphorisms" and Bible texts to deal with potentially upsetting situations: *"What's for you will not go past you"* and *"What goes around comes around"*. Whether you do this or not, can you see how this strategy avoids the problem rather than deals with it?

7   Jesus said: **I give not as the world gives**. Reflect and meditate on these words. What kind of peace can only Jesus give you?

8   **"How can there be peace," Jehu replied, "as long as all the idolatry and witchcraft of your mother Jezebel abound?"** Why not? What accompanies true peace?

Notes

1 Or, in the Greek original, γνῶθι σεαυτόν (gnothi seauton). It has been attributed to various thinkers, including Heraclitus, Pythagoras and Socrates.

2 *Love the LORD your God with all your heart and with all your soul and with all your strength* – expressing the notion that we have three centers within us which all need to be right with God.
Deuteronomy 6:4

3 Don Richard Riso (1993) *Enneagram Transformations*, Houghton Mifflin, p. 126

4 Marianne Williamson, *A Return to Love*, (1996) Harper Paperbacks, p. 29

Bibliography and further reading

De Mello, Anthony (1990) *Awareness*, Zondervan
This book has become something of a modern classic in the genre. De Mello writes in parables and with warmth and wisdom in short, pithy mini-chapters which are really talks given to retreats. Brilliant.

De Mello, Anthony (1991) *The Way to Love*, Doubleday
More of the same as above, but in a tiny book format.

Holmes, Peter (2005) *Becoming More Human*, Paternoster Press
A rather academic but deeply insightful book about personal transformation from the perspective and with the experience of a Christian pastor and psychologist. Sometimes brilliant and enlightening, this book repays study if you are up to the challenge!

Lapid-Bogda, Ginger (2004) *Bringing Out the Best in Yourself at Work*, McGraw-Hill
Dr. Lapid–Bogda writes with clarity and wisdom in a highly-structured and very valuable resource book. Very useful for managers and for dealing with difficult people.

Nouwen, Henri (1994) *The Wounded Healer*, Darton, Longman and Todd
Nouwen's approach was strikingly different from that of many professionals: he argued that professional detachment is a problem, not a solution. His lucid and deeply-felt book arose from a conviction that caring professionals should begin with their own inner hurt. Deep.

Nouwen, Henri (1997) *The Inner Voice of Love*, Darton, Longman and Todd
A short and powerful journal which Nouwen kept during a very difficult and painful time of change and loss of a relationship. It has a raw and angry quality which arises from Nouwen's very genuine struggle with faith, purpose and identity itself.

Peck, M. Scott (1978) *The Road Less Traveled*, Touchstone

Dr. Scott Peck was a psychiatrist who refused to distinguish between spiritual and mental health and growth. I find the book patchy, but its good parts are worth it: he combines long psychiatric experience with a passion for spirituality and personal development.

Riso, Don Richard and Hudson, Russ (1999) *The Wisdom of the Enneagram*, Bantam books

For many, this is the 'Bible' of the Enneagram of personality. Each type is outlined in depth, and there are frequent passages of brilliant insight. The Riso-Hudson approach is profound, deeply spiritual and thoroughly practical. This book will probably still be considered indispensable in 50 years' time.

Riso, Don Richard (1993) *Enneagram Transformations*, Houghton Mifflin

A little gem of a book consisting mostly of mantra-like statements for each type as a practical help towards growth and freedom. The five pages of the last chapter, on healing, are full of rich wisdom.

Rohr, Richard (1995) *Enneagram II*, Fowler Wright books

Rohr is a Franciscan speaker and writer on the Enneagram who brings psychology and Christian faith together in a powerful and challenging way. Sometimes slightly wordy, this is nonetheless a wonderful contribution to the debate and a great help for Christians seeking to grow in faith and personal awareness.

BOOKS

O is a symbol of the world, of oneness and unity. In different cultures it also means the "eye," symbolizing knowledge and insight. We aim to publish books that are accessible, constructive and that challenge accepted opinion, both that of academia and the "moral majority."

Our books are available in all good English language bookstores worldwide. If you don't see the book on the shelves ask the bookstore to order it for you, quoting the ISBN number and title. Alternatively you can order online (all major online retail sites carry our titles) or contact the distributor in the relevant country, listed on the copyright page.

See our website **www.o-books.net** for a full list of over 500 titles, growing by 100 a year.

And tune in to myspiritradio.com for our book review radio show, hosted by June-Elleni Laine, where you can listen to the authors discussing their books.

MySpiritRadio